LORD,

MAKE *My* LIFE

a MIRACLE!

RAY & ANNE
ORTLUND

LORD,
MAKE *My* LIFE
a MIRACLE!

AUTHORS CHOICE PRESS
NEW YORK   BLOOMINGTON

Lord, Make My Life a Miracle!

The views expressed in this work are solely those of the author and do not necessarily reflect the views of the publisher, and the publisher hereby disclaims any responsibility for them.

Authors Choice Press
an imprint of iUniverse, Inc.

iUniverse books may be ordered through booksellers or by contacting:

iUniverse
1663 Liberty Drive
Bloomington, IN 47403
www.iuniverse.com
1-800-Authors (1-800-288-4677)

Because of the dynamic nature of the Internet, any Web addresses or links contained in this book may have changed since publication and may no longer be valid.

ISBN: 978-1-4401-9717-8 (sc)

Printed in the United States of America

iUniverse rev. date: 3/11/2010

CONTENTS

Commitment Three:
Commit Yourself to This Needy World / 107

PREFACE

"Jabez had his prayer, and Ray Ortlund has his," I said as Ray and I sat at dinner with Gary Terashita, our Broadman and Holman editor. I was trying to convince both of them that Ray alone should be named as the author of the revised edition of this book, as he was of the original.

"'Lord, make my life a miracle!'" I quoted and spread out my hands on the table. "It's the cry of us all, when you think about it—but it's been Ray's specific prayer for most of his adult life. The author of this book should still be only Ray.

"Of course I'll work on the revision with him behind the scenes—that's our style. We've done all of our twenty-six books together whether they've been his, mine, or ours. But this prayer is Ray's prayer.

"When he titled this book [which was his first] almost thirty years ago with this personal prayer of his, it sold hundreds of thousands of copies.

"When he became more known as the 'Haven of Rest' radio speaker, our son-in-law Walt Harrah, head of the music, made it into a song, 'Make My Life a Miracle,' which the quartet has sung many times on the program.

"When four hundred dear people put on a surprise party to honor Ray's being in the ministry forty years, on a huge banner that ran the length of one wall was 'Lord, Make My Life a Miracle!' He's identified with the book; he's identified with the prayer.

"And the first part of this book is all Ray's story—the story of his struggle as a pastor to see our church become a miracle, come to genuine spiritual renewal—and the story of God's using Ray's focus on the three priorities to bring that about. It's not _our_ story; it's _his_ story. It's not _our_ book; it's _his_ book."

I had the feeling I'd presented my case well.

Dear Ray! He began gently but firmly eroding my case. (He loves to have me involved in his life.) Across the table, Gary watched our verbal sparring, and at one point he put his napkin up in front of his face.

The exchange was soon over. It was clearly two against one, and so you see on the cover, "Ray and Anne Ortlund." Well, it's true that one of the many ways God is making Ray's life a miracle is the way He has strongly, graciously, tenderly forged our two lives together until we can hardly tell where one life ends and the other begins.

The first two priorities in this book are virtually unchanged from the original. But we both felt the third priority needed more biblical teaching we've learned along the way, plus many exciting practical applications of it that we've seen with our own eyes.

God also has in mind different ways—wonderful ways—to make your own life, reader—friend—a miracle! A generation ago the three priorities spelled out in this book were grabbed by almost a million readers. But it's a new day, and most of our present generation doesn't know them.

They're as biblical as ever.

They're as relevant as ever.

They're more needed than ever!

We invite you to read these pages and make these priorities your own. And then pray for yourself: "Lord, I have only this one earthly life. Help me to 'eliminate and concentrate' . . .

"Lord, make my life a miracle!"

ANNE ORTLUND

THE STORY

*I*t was the fall of the year—new beginning time—and I was pastor of Lake Avenue Congregational Church in Pasadena, California. We were going through all the proper motions of a Great Evangelical Church. Visitors would murmur all the right words about "great missionary emphasis" and "great youth program."

But my heart wasn't satisfied. There were too few "delivery-room" cries of newborns, too few victory songs at midnight.

I had exclaimed in anguish many times in my life, "I refuse to be an ordinary Christian!"

I had pounded the pulpit and said, "I refuse to be an ordinary pastor! I refuse to pastor an ordinary church!"

Then I read a sentence from Thomas Kelly that set my heart on fire. He prayed, "Lord, make my life a miracle."

O God! That's it! You're the God of miracles, and I live in You. Why shouldn't my life be a miracle? Why shouldn't I be able to show others how to be miracles?

I gathered some close brothers and sisters around to pray. To brainstorm. To shoulder my burden with me. (How I loved those people! How willing and ready they were!)

We talked of dissolving the church membership and asking everyone who meant business to join again. (Like at the Battle of the Alamo: "Who will step over this line?")

We met week after week, with lots of ideas. Lots of sawdust and a little gold!

But our God is a God of miracles. "Call to me and I will answer you," He says, "and tell you great and unsearchable things you do not know" (Jer. 33:3).

A few weeks later, on the first Sunday of October, I said to our people attending the early church service, "I have a plan." And I preached on that plan. I concluded with something like this: "We need to turn a new corner. We need a fresh start together as a people. Would you join me in three commitments? I'll be the first to sign my name:

"*Number One:* at whatever stage you are spiritually, commit your heart anew to the Person of God Himself in Jesus Christ. And make that measurable by committing yourself to have a 'quiet time' with Him every day between now and next Easter.

"*Number Two:* commit yourself to the Body of Christ, to be in a regular small group of believers, small enough so that you can be personally accountable to them for your growth and personally responsible for their growth. And make this commitment measurable by choosing three to five people to meet with weekly between now and next Easter. I'll give you seven days to find each other, and we'll gather here in the sanctuary sitting in our new groups next Sunday afternoon at three o'clock.

"*Number Three:* commit yourself to the world, to your work in this world, and to your witness to it. *Make it specific enough* to vow to love one person to Jesus and into the fellowship of the church by next Easter."

Then I said, "If you're willing to commit yourself to these three priorities in this order, sign your name to it on the registration card."

Before the second service, God gave me a name for the signers, borrowed from Elton Trueblood: we'd call them the "Company of the Committed." Bless 'em, the people in the first service didn't even know what they'd joined.

Nobody except my wife, Anne, knew that I'd been desperate enough to make a deal with God. "Lord, if five hundred people don't sign up for this, I'm leaving Lake Avenue Church."

Monday is our day off. I'm not supposed to be around the church at all, but . . .

Did I have a job, or didn't I?

I sneaked into the office of Virginia, my secretary. She grinned. "How about this stack of joiners of the Company of the Committed?" The pile of cards looked gorgeous to me! There were six hundred.

What does God do through the little act of people putting their names on white cards?

It seems like nothing. But then, so does piling up a heap of stones or killing a lamb for sacrifice. . . .

The forming of the Company of the Committed at Lake Avenue Church became a wide-running current of warmth and vitality through the river of the church membership. It was such a widening band that after a few years we quit talking about the Company of the Committed. Lake Avenue Church had *become* a Company of the Committed. Sure, there were ebbs and flows, and, sure, we had lots of fringers, hangers-on, and novices on their way to getting into the Company of the Committed. But our One-Two-Three commitment was the lifestyle of the Body—the lifestyle of many hundreds of turned-on Christians within the Body.

The three commitments seem so simple, but living them out is revolutionary. They're biblical, timeless, transcultural, and basic.

They represent the most exciting concept I know, one that can change your life as it has mine. It says, "My three life priorities are going to be . . .

   1. Christ,

   2. the Body of Christ, and

   3. the world for whom Christ died.

In that order!"

In this book, let me show you what I mean.

COMMITMENT ONE:

Commit Your Heart Again to God

"Yes, yes," you say hastily, "I accepted Christ when I was twelve, and that's already settled. Now let's get on to the Body, to fellowship, to marriage and family, to lifestyle, to all these fun things everybody's chatting about these days."

Wait! Stop! Be still! Be quiet!

You're nearsighted, my friend. Your eyes are focused on what's closest. So are the eyes of millions of other busy, nervous, frantic, activist Christians in this age.

Will you adjust your vision? Will you look beyond all that? Will you see the Lord, high and lifted up, seated on His throne, surrounded by worshiping ones? Will you dare to lift your eyes?

You'll be smitten. You'll realize you're profane. You'll be separated from all your busy-busy, horizontally motivated brothers. You'll cry, "O God, my mouth is filthy, and I live among people with filthy mouths. I'm undone" (Isa. 6:5 paraphrased).

But oh, my friend! The sight of this Super Being will not crush you, but cleanse you. His fire will burn away all your filthiness, all your bitterness. (Yes, I'm talking to Christians.)

You'll feel so free, so clean, so exhilarated that when you hear God's challenge for service, you'll be ready for

Number Two: attention to the Body, and

Number Three: attention to your work in this world.

Don't rush past Number One.

This is the Blockbuster.

This, my Christian friend, may be your personal confrontation on the Damascus road.

chapter one
LIVE WITH GOD

*W*hen Galileo discovered the truth of the earth's center, it caused all science to make some revisions. All that had been previously believed had to be adjusted to this new fact.

When you begin to see that the true center of life is in God, then all the rest of your life must be adjusted to that new and true fact.

Someone said that the most fundamental thing anyone can do is to bring a person to God and leave him there. That's my desire! I want to get to God and stay there, and I want this also for you.

Thomas Kelly wrote: "We are unhappy, uneasy, strained, oppressed, and fearful we shall be shallow. Over the margins of life comes a whisper, a faint call, a premonition of richer living which we know we are passing by. . . . We have hints that there is a way of life vastly richer and deeper than all this hurried existence, a life of unhurried serenity and peace and power. If only we could slip over into that Center! If only we could find the Silence which is the source of sound!"[1]

One summer on vacation I had stumbled onto the writing of this Thomas Kelly, a recent Quaker. He was saying things my heart responded to, things I wasn't hearing from other modern-day evangelicals. I traced the people he quoted—George Fox and other early Quakers, clear back to writers in the thirteenth and fourteenth centuries.

I had always *believed* in the centrality of God; I had taught the doctrine of it. There are many authors who take this doctrine as their central theme and do a beautiful job with it—J. I. Packer, John Piper, and others. But to find those who talk about the *techniques* of living consciously "in God," you must go back to the old church fathers—or to someone like Brother Lawrence *(The Practice of the Presence of God²)*—or you go to the Quakers.

You see, today we are activists. We love Christ, but we don't stay much around Him. We talk gladly of God's forgiveness, but we don't have too much time to wait on Him or for Him or with Him. We are on the move. We run into prayer, and then too quickly we say, "I've got to get on with life, with real life."

How unaware we are of what "the real" really is!

In the fall we see flocks of geese heading south. They may land on a pond and feed for awhile; but soon, however pleasant that surrounding may be, there is an instinct that calls them out into the blue and down to the South. It calls them to their home.

Christian friend, do you feel in your heart a new tugging toward God? Do you feel that longing instinct, that you're not—in your day-by-day experience—all the way home yet? God is stirring you up; He's moving you. Up out of the pond! Keep pursuing!

After Thomas Kelly, I ran across the writings of Frank Laubach, in a little book called *Letters by a Modern Mystic*. This "turned me on" some more about this, and I began to really see that in my own personal life there had been much lack. Frank Laubach was a missionary in the Philippines who, by the way, saw that millions were taught to read. This man wrote,

> For the past few days I have been experimenting
> in a more complete surrender than ever before. I am
> taking, by deliberate act of the will, enough time from

each hour to give God much thought. Yesterday and today I have made a new adventure, which is not easy to express. I am feeling God in each movement, by an act of will.

You will object to this intense introspection. Do not try it, unless you feel dissatisfied with your own relationship with God, but at least allow me to realize all the leadership of God I can. I am disgusted with the pettiness and futility of my unled self. If the way out is not more perfect slavery to God, then what is the way out?

Paul speaks of our liberty in Christ. I am trying to be utterly free from everybody, free from my own self, but completely enslaved to the will of God every moment of this day.[3]

I've been living this recently with much failure and, now and then, a little bit of success. I use an alarm wristwatch that I was given by dear Wycliffe missionaries in Vietnam after ministering there. I set my alarm every fifteen minutes just to remind myself, _It's time, boy, to become aware again, to reach. Draw near and enjoy the presence of God. Don't get bogged down with everything around you._ This is what my alarm is for, and when it doesn't bother others, I set it.

But I find I don't need it so much now because the Holy Spirit has been wonderful in helping me to be aware of God.

You know, there were a couple of sins in my life that I couldn't break. I really couldn't! They were mastering me. But when I find myself in the presence of God, those sins don't belong. It's amazing what the presence of God does. He makes those things incompatible with Himself; they're not important anymore, and they've lost their hold on me.

Praise God!

Sin will keep you from God's presence, or God's presence will keep you from sin.

Jesus began His earthly life based on the promise "God is with us" (Matt. 1:23). He ended His earthly life with the promise, "I am with you always" (Matt. 28:20). At both ends, the promise of the Presence.

And not just the Presence *with,* but the Presence *within.* As the infant Saviour was placed into Mary and formed in her womb, so Paul cries out in Galatians, "I am in the pains of childbirth for you until Christ is formed in you!" (4:19). You commit your body to Him that you might become His temple, the housing of God Himself—"Christ in you, the hope of glory" (Col. 1:27).

There is so much that's rich here. I feel as though I'm barely touching on it. But God calls us to live *with Him.* This is not the idea of the omnipresence of God. It isn't the idea that I invited Jesus to come into my heart. That's wonderful, and the omnipresence of God is wonderful, but that's not what I'm talking about.

I'm talking about consciously, continually, living in the presence of God. Going in and out and finding pasture, as it were. Talking with Him, enjoying Him, loving Him—rejoicing, praising, crying, complaining—all those things, in the presence of God.

Strong's *Systematic Theology* makes this comment: "The majority of Christians much more frequently think of Christ as a Saviour *outside of them* than as a Saviour who dwells within."[4]

We think of Christ as in heaven, 'way up there.

Now here is our desk with a pile of papers we are trying to go through, while the phone is ringing off the hook.

Or the kitchen has to be cleaned, and somebody just spilled orange juice on the floor, and we've got to go get groceries.

Or we're in a classroom, and there's a paper due tomorrow morning or it's one point off our grade.

There are so many immediate *now* problems, and they get first "dibs" on our attention because *we think our problems are closer to us than Christ!* We haven't yet learned that "in Him we live and move and exist" (Acts 17:28). We don't understand that He is closer than hands or feet. We haven't yet learned to *live from the inside out.*

My friend, *Christ is in you* far more really, far more present, than all that which is going on around you! He is closer than any problem! If you are living moment by moment with this great awareness of God within, everything else will be truly revolutionized.

Within! Within!

Most Christians would say, "Of course I know He's there." But educators say we haven't really learned something until there's changed behavior.

When Jacob ran from Esau, he slept that night and had a great dream. When he woke up, he exclaimed, "Surely the LORD is in this place, and I did not know it"! (Gen. 28:16 NASB).

Is that really true—experientially true—with you? Jacob was so engrossed with his problems with his brother, and he was pell-mell on the run. Through a dream, God brought him up short—to see Himself.

Maybe for you—through these words?

It could be that you're feeling frustrated, that this sounds fine but it's just an unattainable goal because there are so many demands upon your life. Maybe someday when you retire; but right now, you feel so pulled, so splintered.

Thomas Kelly says, "We are trying to be several selves all at once, without all of our selves being organized by a single, mastering life within us. Each of us tends to be, not a single self, but a whole committee of selves. There is the civic self, the parental self, the financial self, the religious self, the society self, the professional self, the literary self."[5]

But God calls us first of all to Himself. There we find integration; we find unity; we find simplicity. One Lord, one faith, one baptism! There is a singularity about Him, and there must also be a singularity about the life that is lived *in Him.*

Kelly goes on: "I think it is clear that I am talking about a revolutionary way of living. Practicing the Presence isn't something to be added to our many other duties, and thus make our lives yet more complex. The life with God is the center of life, and all else is remodeled and integrated by it."

Everything is at hand, right here at the center. All power, all peace, all wisdom for moment-by-moment choices. We're moving into the practical, nitty-gritty how-to of the established fact of the indwelling of the Holy Spirit. When you catch it, you'll live from the center out rather than from the outside in.

When you live from the outside in, what happens to you inside? You get all tense and tied up. You're like a boxer waiting for the next punch. You're living, reacting to one situation, then reacting to the next one, and so on—happy or unhappy depending on each external circumstance.

What a shame! That's no different from the way an atheist lives!

George Fox wrote: "It is a wonderful discovery to find that you are a temple, that you have a church inside of you, where God is. In hushed silence, attend to Him. 'The Lord is in His holy temple!'"[6]

King David said to young Mephibosheth, "You and Ziba divide the land between you."

And Mephibosheth answered, "Look, let Ziba take all the land. Let me just live with you, David, and eat at your table. That's all I want!" (See 2 Sam. 19:29–30; also 2 Sam. 2:7–11).

Oh, that's the way to be! Longing for God Himself! Nothing but God. That's why God could use Moses: Moses cried, "I don't want angels, I don't want substitutes, I just want God!"

If you don't know the "hereness" of God—then, my friend, you haven't begun to find out His relevance for your moment-by-moment life.

But as for me, it is good to be near God.
I have made the Sovereign LORD my refuge.
(Ps. 73:28)

In thy presence is fullness of joy; at thy right hand there are pleasures for evermore. (Ps. 16:11 KJV)

God said to Moses, "My Presence will go with you, and I will give you rest." (Exod. 33:14)

Oh, the joy, the comfort of living with God! Dear friend, don't miss it!

This isn't a single commitment; it's a one-moment-at-a-time commitment. It calls you from "scattered-mindedness" to single-mindedness.

How long are the great masses of God's people going to be preoccupied with the fringes, the externals, the side issues?

God is so patient. Think how many times He has flashed lightning across the sky. Through the ages it would splinter huge trees. It would run a cow down a path while people watched and wondered.

All the time God was trying to tell them something.

One stormy day a man finally went out with a kite and a key. All heaven was probably bending over saying, "All these years we've been trying to tell them about electricity. Look, look, he's got it! At last, he's got it!" And soon the world lit up.

How long, how long you and I have been vaguely aware—theoretically aware—of God's presence with us! I think all heaven's been waiting, and perhaps saying, "I think they might get it. Look, look, maybe at last they're going to get it!"

Christian, you may have been saved for fifteen, thirty, forty years. Maybe at last you're going to get it!

The Christian life is to be lived from the center out, with God. How could you have missed it? At the center is Jesus Christ and all His glory in you.

Begin the sweet discipline of acknowledging Him, moment by moment. Live with Him, have a running conversation going with Him, rejoice in Him.

Have you got it?[7]

chapter two
BE
GOD-CENTERED

T.J. Bach was the leader of the Evangelical Alliance Mission, and one of the great Christians of this past century. He so lived in the presence of God that he would just be in and out of God's presence as he was in and out of the presence of other people.

Some of the men of our church were recounting stories of him the other morning. If you said to Dr. Bach, "I think I'm going to town this afternoon," he would say, "Lord, bless my friend as he goes to town. What time are you going?"

None of this bow-your-head-close-your-eyes-fold-your-hands sort of thing. He was just talking, and God was in it all.

You say, "But isn't that really kind of eccentric?"

Well, let's think about what it means to be eccentric. Your life is like a wheel. At your center, your hub, is the indwelling Christ. The hub is the place of control, of stillness and yet power. The first line in an old hymn is

There is a place of quiet rest
Near to the heart of God.

14

The rim is where your life touches all that's outside of you: the people in your life, your situations, good news, bad news, world affairs. The rim is the part that goes the fastest, and it's where all the heat and dust and friction are.

And, Christian, from moment to moment you have a choice: whether to live in constant awareness of your rim (living from the outside in and being happy or sad, up or down, depending on what's going on around you) or whether to live in constant awareness of your quiet, powerful hub (living from the inside out: "Lord what do we do next? Make me godly with this person. . . . I trust you to handle that situation through me. . . .").

Thomas Kelly, a recent Quaker, says this: "On one level we may be . . . meeting all the demands of the external affairs. But deep within, behind the scenes, at a profounder level, one may also be in prayer and adoration, song and worship, and a gentle receptiveness to divine breathings."[1]

So, Christian, you have a choice: you can be God-centered—Christocentric—or you can be eccentric. The eccentric man is the man who is a bit off center. How does he get that way? He will be eccentric if anything but God is central.

Anything but God.

Now, you want a Christian life that's meaningful. What is it that will help you have a meaningful life? You say, "Well, I'll go to a good, sound church. Surely this is the way to purpose and satisfaction."

You find a church and it's exciting. Things are happening. A bright, happy spirit is there; God is at work. You say, "This is it!"

You throw yourself into committees and boards and Sunday school classes—but after a year or two you say, "Well, a lot of these people are no better than I am, and some of them have worse problems than I have."

At this point you get restless again. It doesn't mean you leave the church, but you begin to look for something else, something deeper. . . .

You hear of a special doctrine held by some people who meet in a home and listen to somebody's tapes, and you think, _Why haven't I heard of this before? How come no one has told me about this?_ And you say, "Soul, rejoice! Your search is over. This is it!"

So your life focuses on this new doctrine, this specialization. And it's wonderful; it's biblical. But soon you find that it doesn't really take care of everything, and you're still restless in your soul. You feel dry and empty.

Then one day a friend who seems to be full of joy says to you, "What you really need is a certain Christian experience." You think, _That must be true. That's exactly what I need._ So you go to the place where these people are having this experience, and they all seem happy and rejoicing; and you say, "Hallelujah! This is _it!_"

And you try to get "it," too, and all the group urges you on. They're rooting for you—and they say, "You've got to have more faith. Let go! Give up! Relax!"

Finally you get "it." You have this great experience, and you say, "This has to be it. This must be it!"

Eventually the old restlessness creeps back.

Why?

Because all the time you were looking for _it,_ and not for _Him!_

You see, the church itself must never be "front and center" in your life. Neither should an experience—you mustn't be experience-centered. A specialization or true, good doctrine must never be central. _God Himself_ must be central. Anything else will make you eccentric—off center.

Here's a factory. All over it are wheels—huge wheels, little wheels, medium wheels—and they are all turning. The factory is running, and everything runs smoothly because all the wheels are on center.

Here's another factory, with good wheels, well-made wheels, important wheels—but each wheel is just a bit off center. When that factory begins to operate at 7:30 on a Monday morning, look out! There'll be all kinds of clattering and squeaking and smells of burning bearings. The place is shaking to pieces!

You know, this factory is like many a church. Everyone is doing his "thing."

There's a wheel over here squeaking away, saying, "You've got to witness. Everybody's got to witness."

And there's another wheel smoking away, saying, "You've got to get into contemporary worship!" Around it goes: "Contemporary worship, contemporary worship, contemporary worship!"

Another wheel over here is groaning, "Second coming, second coming, second coming" and another, "Missions, missions, missions. . . ."

Now, all of their emphases are right and good, but if they're central, those Christians are eccentric! No wonder the average church is full of bumping and jostling.

How can you tell if you're eccentric? Well, examine yourself. If you follow any leader, any movement, any church, any doctrine, and make this central to your life and thinking, my friend, you're eccentric. You're spiritually off balance.

Second Corinthians 5:14–15 is so important. It says that Christ "died for all so that those who live should no longer live for themselves, but *for the One who died for them and was raised.*"

God alone is the balanced Person. God the Father, God the Son, God the Holy Spirit—They alone are really one, unified, whole. God alone is sufficient in Himself. And we have been so constructed as His people that we are only whole, we are only sufficient, when all our lives are revolving around Him. We must be God-centered.

Many Christians are living lopsided lives. Their lives are indeed that wheel, but with too much attention given to this or that part of the circumference, the rim. They're occupied with what's *outside* of them instead of occupied with God Who is that "Holy Within." *He* must be the hub, the focus, the purpose.

This calls for a "centralized government" in your life. In Matthew 6:33 Jesus is talking about all the circumference things of life—food, clothing, and so on—and He says, "Seek first the kingdom of God [the government of Christ], and all these things will be provided for you."

David wrote, "As the deer pants for streams of water, so my soul pants for you, O God" (Ps. 42:1).

"So that," wrote Paul, "He might come to have first place in everything" (Col. 1:18).

Does something tug at you that says, "Oh, but surely I can have the best of two worlds—all of the circumference and God at the hub too"?

When Francis of Assisi was a young man, it was said of him that when other young men ran away to the world, he ran away to God. No wonder everyone is still quoting him, singing his songs.

Hebrews 11:6 tells us, "He that cometh to God must believe that he is, and that *he is a rewarder of them that diligently seek him*" (KJV).

My Christian friend, if you have not diligently sought after God in your life, really gone hard after God, to make Him central, to give Him preeminence—it may be because deep down, deep down in your heart, *you do not believe* that He is the rewarder of those who seek Him.

The big lie from the world and from the pit of hell itself is that God is not a good rewarder, that if you really follow hard after Him, you'll miss some of the "kicks" of life, some of the "goodies."

You've been sold a bill of goods.

Only in God, *only in God* is there reward. Hear it—only in God.

Isaiah 26:3 says this to you:

You will keep in perfect peace
    him whose mind is steadfast,
    because he trusts in you.

That's "practicing the Presence," my friend. That's holding God in central place in your heart.

And here's another snare: Even as we think about being God-centered, our tendency is to want it "for me"—so I can have this "perfect peace"—and "I" am still in the center! I want the experience because it will make me a top-quality, grade-A Christian on the top of the pile—and at that point God is not attended to and waited upon and sought for what He is.

Oh, our motives, our motives!

But let me tell you something: you were made for God. You can go on lopsided through life if you want to, banging and squeaking on your way; that's your choice. But you were made to have Christ at the center. Christ in you alone glorifies God and truly satisfies you.

Augustine said, "Our hearts are restless, O God, until they rest in Thee."

Christian, you can choose to invite God into the very center of your life and let life flow outward from that inner core. You can "center down," as the Quakers say, on God Himself, if you want to—so that Christ becomes absolutely everything to you. God, the Holy Spirit, is in you to pull that off.

That's what F. W. M. Myers did, that he could write,

Christ's! I am Christ's!

And let the name suffice you.

Aye, and for me

He greatly hath sufficed.[2]

This is how it affected one humble London tailor, John Woolman, many centuries ago: "When too many customers came, he sent them elsewhere, to more needy merchants and tailors. His outward life became simplified on the basis of an inner integration. He found that we can be heavenly men and women, and he surrendered himself completely, unreservedly, to that blessed leading, keeping warm and close to the Center."[3]

George Fox, the founder of Quakerism in the 1600s, had this kind of itch for God: not to know religion but God in Christ Himself. He went everywhere seeking from ministers, priests, and laymen—anyone who could possibly tell him how he might know God.

His relatives said, "What you need, George, is to get married."

A priest advised him to smoke tobacco and to sing psalms.

Another minister got angry and wouldn't even answer him because he stepped in his flower bed.

Another told him that what he really needed was some medicine and a good bloodletting!

Obviously, seminary training didn't hold the answer. Eventually Fox came to write, "Unless you know God, immediately, every day communing with Him, rejoicing in Him, exulting in Him, opening your life in joyful obedience toward Him, and feeling Him speaking to you and guiding you into ever fuller obedience to Him—you aren't fit to be a minister."[4] (Or, I might say, even to be a Christian.)

Now, this takes faith. "That [He] may dwell in your hearts through faith," says Paul in Ephesians 3:17. He means that the indwelling Christ and the enjoyment of Him continually requires an attitude of believing, an attitude of faith—that you really stay close to where the action is.

It's in God, my friend! It isn't anywhere else. That's "where it is"—in God.

You don't have to keep tabs on the Christian fire—defending it, fanning it—lest it go out. My friend, the fire is God. You only need to keep close to the fire. So do I.

Only those who know God, who get with God, who go with God in their daily life experiences, ever get to know the elegance of God.

Centuries ago, Brother Lawrence was a young man who was crippled. He went into a monastery so that he might somehow atone for the fact that he was such a clumsy person.

But he was hungry for God. In the monastery he was put to work washing the floors and pots and pans of the kitchen. And it was he who in the midst of this "practiced the presence of God." Brother Lawrence said, "For me the time of action does not differ from the time of prayer, and in the noise and clatter of my kitchen, while several persons are calling for as many different things, I possess God in as great tranquility as when upon my knees."[5]

When he was dying, during long stretches of silence on his bed his friends asked him what he was doing. He replied, "I am doing what I shall do through all eternity—blessing God, praising God, adoring God, giving Him the love of my whole heart. It is our one business, my brethren, to worship Him and love Him, without thought of anything else."[6]

If you are seeking a richer life, as I'm sure you are, you want something grander for the future than you've known in the past. God bless you! That's the hunger for God put in your heart by Him.

Listen, be like the disciples! You have toiled all night and taken nothing (see John 21:3). Now let down your nets. Go after Him. Go into the deeps.

And how do you do it? Well, just begin right where you are.

Inwardly begin to adore God. Begin to praise Him at the very depths of your being. Right now just say, "Lord, I love You. I praise You. I admire You! I want to live in Your presence."

Tomorrow morning when you get up, say, "Lord, here we are. What are we going to do today? I want to be with You all day long."

Fairer than morning,
Lovelier than daylight
Dawns the sweet consciousness—
I am with Thee![7]

Then all day long, behind the scenes, at the very deepest level, hold conversations with God.

As you walk down the street, ask God's blessing on those you see.

As you stop at a stoplight, express your love to Jesus.

As you go into your own home: "Dear God, today will You bless this home—and me, as I go in."

And as you go from here to there: "Praise to God. Your will be done."

Keep the conversation running. It will take no extra time, my friend. It will take *all* your time.

And when you fail?—when you get clever again? when you assert your own way? Well, don't spend lots of time groveling over it. Get up and go on. Go to God, and get on with Him again.

We are so success-centered, it's hard to have the patience to develop this quality of life. On our television programs, every mystery is solved in just twenty-eight minutes. And all the laundry problems are solved in sixty seconds!

But living with God takes time. Perhaps you have gray hairs and have lived long with the Lord; you know it takes time to grow deep with God. Oh, you need to keep at it. You're not home yet. Keep there, keep in close, dear older friend. Know what it is to grow old graciously in the presence of the Lord. You'll succeed! Oh, I've failed so often. But the little bit of success I know is too good to give up.

This is not a self-improvement scheme. It isn't for you; this is for God! This is to gather ourselves around Him, and give Him glory and pleasure. This is the *God*-centered life.

What if you sin? You go to His presence anyway. Brother Lawrence said, "Lord, I'll keep doing the same thing all the time, unless You help me."

Confess that sin, and then relax. "For it is God who is working among you," says Philippians 2:13, "both the willing and the working for His good purpose."

Think a minute about T. J. Bach. He was the only one who was *on* center! The world around him thought he was eccentric. My friend, *they* were the eccentric ones!

Do you fear becoming fanatic? It's true that you won't be following a huge crowd if you live this way. But Thomas Kelly said, "Better to run the possible risk of fanaticism by complete dedication to God than to run the certain risk of mediocrity by 20 percent dedication. Better to run the risk of being examined by a psychiatrist than to measure our lives by our mediocre fellows. The prophets come to the world and say, 'Thus saith the Lord.' They don't say, 'Thus saith the majority'!"[8]

My Christian friend, I call you to God.[9]

chapter three

WORSHIP IN PRIVATE

*T*here's one prime, basic, all-important place in your life where the rubber really meets the road. At this place, my friend, you win or lose—you make it or you don't.

The place I'm talking about is where you go down on your knees, where you shut out all the rest of the world, and where you and God—just the two of you—get together.

It has to be honest between you and Him.

It has to be regular, at least once a day.

And it has to be fought for, clawed and scratched for—or it will never happen.

As sweet as life is to live with God moment by moment—and that's where it all begins—that doesn't rule out your need for a consistent "quiet time," a tryst with Him for Bible study and prayer.

George Mueller, the man of great faith in nineteenth-century England, shared how he found the secret of his spiritual power: "The first thing to be concerned about was not how much I might serve the Lord, but how I might get my soul into a happy state, and how my inner man might be nourished. . . . I began therefore to meditate on the New Testament from the beginning, early in the morning. The first thing I did, after having asked in a few words the Lord's blessing upon His precious Word, was to begin to meditate on the Word of God, searching out of it, not for the sake of public ministry of the Word, not for the sake of preaching on what I had meditated upon, but for obtaining for my own soul."[1]

You don't get food for your soul by osmosis! You can hear others talk of it; but until you yourself regularly take in that delicious Word of God, you're undernourished!

It was important for Christ. That in itself should make us go after quiet times with God. Think of it: Jesus took large hunks of time to be alone with His Father: "Very early in the morning, while it was still dark, He got up, went out, and made His way to a deserted place. And He was praying there" (Mark 1:35). Evidently even the eternal Christ needed quiet periods of prayer. "He often withdrew to deserted places and prayed" (Luke 5:16).

How nice of the Holy Spirit: He encourages us to spend time alone with God by showing us that Jesus did it!

It's not easy for us to comprehend, of course. Jesus is the Son of God; why was it necessary? He was "with God; [He] was God" (see John 1:1). But He "practiced the presence of God" in that utter and complete way that Psalm 16:8–11 prophesied:

I have set the LORD always before me
[says the Son, talking about the Father].
 Because he is at my right hand,
 I will not be shaken.
Therefore my heart is glad and my
  tongue rejoices;
 my body also will rest secure,
because you will not abandon me to the grave,
 nor will you let your Holy One see decay.

Listen to this final verse in the King James Version:
Thou wilt shew me the path of life: in thy presence is fulness of joy; at thy right hand there are
pleasures for evermore.

Even though He lived and moved and existed in God (see
Acts 17:28) in a unique way, Jesus still had to get away for quiet.
He had to shut out the world for large hunks of time and com-
municate with the Father with no interruptions.

You say, "But He didn't live in the twenty-first century!" My
friend, we all have the time we need for what we really want most
to do.

Choose a quiet place and a particular time for this daily event.
You may not be able to keep the schedule every day, but work at
it. Anytime becomes no time. Fix a daily appointment with God.
Write it into your date book!

If I sound like the professional who's had all this mastered for
years, let me tell you: Ray Ortlund sweats it out. There are plenty
of pressures on a minister's time. Through the years I've wavered
back and forth between frustration and some success.

A few months ago I got good and desperate (I think God
loves that!) and said, "OK, Lord, it's going to be 5:15 every morning. That sounds like a time when there should be a minimum of
visitors and phone interruptions."

Ugh! Do you know what the world looks like at 5:15 A.M.?

Do you know how hideous an alarm can sound then?

Do you know how luscious the bed feels at that hour?

Before long I knew that the secret of getting up early was
going to bed early! That's not easy in these crazy days. But here's
where I had to plan my week with care. If meeting with God was
top priority, then other events would have to fit in, after, and
around. Period!

I began with "gusto." It was good. It was so rewarding that
even the problem of afternoon fatigue (and making time for a nap)

was worth the success I enjoyed. Now, six months later, it's not all success—but it's right, and I like it.

Frankly, as I look back over this period, I don't see myself sprouting wings—but, praise God, I do sense He is quietly winning victories in my life. That makes it worth it all.

Whenever God and you are to meet together is up to you and Him. Let me warn you though: when you can't, when you fail to keep the appointment, don't beat yourself for it. After all, who are you to think you can be so perfect or consistent? And who am I? But by His strength, keep at it!

The goal of your Bible reading can be reached by asking the same two questions that Paul asked on the Damascus road:

- "Who are You, Lord?" (Acts 22:8).
- "What should I do, Lord?" (Acts 22:10).

In that holy time before the Book, have a double goal—to know God and to obey Him.

What is the process of getting to this goal? Pray for understanding, and then read through your chosen passage for the day. Ask yourself what you learn in that passage about God or Christ. Don't hurry. Don't quit too soon. "Who are You, Lord?"

Also observe what you see is God's will for you. "What shall I do, Lord?" Then pray it and write it into your day's plans.

Then have a structured, diligent prayer time. When I pray, I like to use the simple acrostic of the word *ACTS:*

A – Adoration

C – Confession

T – Thanksgiving

S – Supplication (for others and yourself)

You learn to pray by praying. Use your head and your heart. When you pray, think! It helps greatly to talk out loud, or else to write down your prayers in a personal notebook. Tell Him your heart's desires. Really work at avoiding clichés! God must get tired of our dull sameness.

I like to plot my day in prayer. The two of us (the Lord and I) run through my appointments together and cover them all, even to the unknown interruptions. When I thank Him for interruptions before they ever happen, I find I handle them better. (They're part of your "Plan A," Father!)

As I was writing this, a pastor friend dropped in. Quiet time in the study is at a premium, but I found our conversation a real delight. What's more, as I committed it all to God while it was happening, he got to the point of his visit right away and I was back to work again. How important it is to hang in there with God and then feel Him enable me to hang loose! It surely beats any other way I know.

A medical doctor friend was on a retreat with our college gang recently. They were studying private prayer and practicing it. As he watched them go hard after God, he said to the minister to students, "If my patients did this, half of them would never need to come to me."

My wife, Anne, and I often feel the need to seek the Lord for a longer period, for a day or part of a day, the two of us alone together with God. We bring our notebooks and our Bibles, and we have a time. Sometimes the mountains call us, sometimes the beach, but we alternate times. We have a day of refreshing in the Word—singing, talking, and praying together and separately.

It's so good to check up on our marriage. "How am I doing as a husband?" She can "shoot straight" in the cushioned atmosphere of prayer. And I can take it without getting uptight. "How do you sense I'm doing in my life with the Lord? How can I improve?"

Try a day of prayer! It's refreshing and lifting. Make your own outline of what you should cover. Choose a Bible passage and work on it; make a list of subjects you need to pray through.

If Jesus did it, certainly we need to!

The psalmist prayed:

Direct me in the path of your commands,
    for there I find delight. . . .

Turn my eyes away from worthless things; . . .
I will walk about in freedom,
>   for I have sought out your precepts.
(119:35, 37, 45)

Oh, the flavoring, the seasoning that God gives to a life shot through with times with Him!

"Observing the boldness of Peter and John and realizing them to be uneducated and untrained men, they were amazed and knew that they had been with Jesus" (Acts 4:13).

Lord, I have shut the door;
>   Speak now the Word
>   Which in the din and throng
>   Could not be heard;
>   Hushed now my inner heart;
>   Whisper Thy will,
>   While I have come apart,
>   While all is still.[2]

It's really up to you. It's where you win or lose.

chapter four
WORSHIP IN PUBLIC

*I*t's like the weather: everybody talks about it, but nobody really does much about it—this matter of worshiping. Thousands go through the motions every Sunday. A few are worshiping; most are just "playing church."

You've got to think about public worship. The task before you, Christian, is to *worship*—every week! Not to go to church every week and have the experience of true worship once a year, or almost never. But every time you go, to have learned the cleansing, satisfying art of public worship.

When Jesus came to earth He announced: "An hour is coming, and is now here, when the true worshipers will worship the Father in spirit and truth. Yes, the Father wants such people to worship Him. God is Spirit, and those who worship Him must worship in spirit and truth" (John 4:23–24).

Worship is the highest and noblest act that any person can do. When men worship, God is satisfied! "The Father is seeking such to worship Him" (John 4:23 NKJV). Amazing, isn't it? And when you worship, you are fulfilled! Think about this: Why did Jesus Christ come? He came to make worshipers out of rebels. We who were once self-centered have to be completely changed so that we can shift our attention outside of ourselves and become able to worship Him.

"It ain't easy!"

Worship is top priority. Everything—absolutely everything—must be put aside to do this thing that God has called you to do. Worship is lofty business—but, friend, we do it so poorly.

I'm amazed at several obvious ways that our poverty in worship is displayed. Many Christians don't even show up with regularity. A person may say, "Well, I just don't get anything out of it."

You get nothing out of it?!

You get nothing out of the Word of the eternal God?!

You get nothing out of the great hymns of the church, or the earnestness of praise songs?!

You get nothing out of prayer through Jesus Christ to God Almighty?!

Then it's because you don't know how to put anything into it. It shows our deep misunderstanding of what worship is all about.

Or a person may say, "I'm tired. It's the only day I have off during the week." Friend, that's the only day you have *on!* You'd better be "on" because worship is the meaning of the whole thing of living. If your job makes you too tired to worship God, quit your job. Find another. But I doubt if that's really your problem.

And here's a subtle thing: our wonderful emphasis on fellowship has contributed to our deep poverty in worship! Think of that! We must cherish fellowship—it's good. But we must continually magnify worship—it's the best, much higher than anything else we can do. Too often we come to meet each other and miss meeting God. We chat with each other, but never really speak to God.

I believe the problem is that we've never really learned the importance of worship. It's never really "come home" to us.

Can you imagine: some even go to some wonderful Bible class, but they don't go to a worship service! This completely amazes me. What if a child spent his entire childhood in his classroom at school with no home, no mother, no deep level of communication, no loving arms?

Something else that shows our poverty in worship is the attitude in which we come. You think it doesn't show? It does! Some come and fold their arms and lean back, look around, and kind of evaluate the situation. "How is the preacher doing today? His trousers are pressed pretty well. How do things look up in the praise band?" Or "in the choir?"

Let me tell you something: you may have been to theological seminary and heard the greatest Bible teachers, but if you don't know how to worship, you haven't yet reached that for which you were made. I really mean that! The so-called "Christian experts" may come to the Bible as an answer book rather than a book to get them to God.

Some Christians may be poor in worship simply because they're young in the Lord. They haven't yet learned the great and wonderful joy of worship. They don't yet know how to press in, press in to the very heart of God and meet Him there. They've come out of the culture that says, "You go to church on Sunday? Man, don't you have any fun?"

My wife, Anne, writes this in her book *Up with Worship:*

In the Bible the word *worship* is variously translated "to bow," "to do reverence to," "to kiss the hand of," or other expressions to indicate an acknowledgment of the presence of Somebody Great. And *God ordained worship* to strengthen our relationship with Him.

God ordained lovemaking too. Think about the similarities.

Here's a wife who says, "Of course I love him! I keep his house and cook his meals, don't I?" But she seldom touches him, and she almost never says, "I love you! You are so precious to me!" There you have a dry, sterile marriage, missing the foundational underpinnings of a satisfying relationship.

Sex is a ritual that God ordained to bind marriage partners together, and He tells us, "Do not deprive each other" (1 Cor. 7:5).

Worship services are a ritual God ordained too—to bind us experientially to Him! Here's a believer who says, "Of course I love the Lord! I sponsor the youth group and teach Sunday school, don't I?" But he is seldom in the worship service, and if he comes he almost never looks right into the face of God and says, "I love You, Lord! You are truly precious to me!" There you have a dry, sterile Christian, missing the foundational underpinnings of a satisfying relationship with God Himself. And so He tells us, "Don't forsake assembling together" (Heb. 10:25 paraphrased).

Do you mind my saying that the two acts, worship and sex, have some similarities?

Both acts must be regular.

Both must be wholehearted.

Both must be top-priority, for which other things are put aside; they're the result of solemn commitment.[1]

People say that sitting in rows in church is so impersonal. That's right! That's good! Jesus took His best friends up the mountain with Him. But then He *withdrew from them a stone's throw* and fell on His face. When you go to worship, go to meet God personally. Whatever anyone else does around you, you get through to Him.

Notice two phrases in John 4: "True worshipers will worship the Father in spirit and truth" (v. 23) and "Those who worship Him must worship in spirit and truth" (v. 24). Twice that formula "spirit and truth" is given. And it says worship is not something we do if we like, but it says "will" and "must"! There are few "musts" in the Bible. Worship is one of them.

Think about it: how do you worship in spirit? That is, how do you worship in the Holy Spirit and in your human spirit as well?

First, it's the Holy Spirit Who prompts you to praise correctly. Ephesians 2:18 in *The Living Bible* says, "Now all of us . . . come to God the Father with the Holy Spirit's help because of what Christ has done for us." The whole Trinity is involved. We get to God on the merits of our Lord Jesus, Saviour, present Master in our lives, and we are helped to do this by the energy and understanding of the Holy Spirit. We worship "in the Spirit."

Oh, how we must have the help of the Holy Spirit if we're going to worship! There is a powerful downward drag inside us because by nature we are not God-centered, but self-centered. We need that prayer from the *Book of Common Worship:* "Almighty God, unto Whom all hearts be open, all desires known, and from Whom no secrets are hid; cleanse the thoughts of our hearts, by the inspiration of Thy Holy Spirit, that we may perfectly love Thee, and worthily magnify Thy Holy Name; through Jesus Christ our Lord."[2]

It's the only way.

Your worship, then, must be by the Holy Spirit.

The externals are not important.

Listen to one more excerpt from Anne's book, *Up with Worship:*

If we could sit at His feet like Mary in Luke 10 and listen to our very own Creator talk to us—this all-wise Ancient of Days,

Who is both scathing in the horror of His white-hot wrath and also achingly tender as a sanctuary for those of us who love Him—

Our Peace, our Truth, our Righteousness, our Hope, our Life—this glorious Majesty, happy, loving, singing, charming, altogether pure, powerfully sustaining all the universe, funny, dear, splendid. . . .

If we could sit there, undistracted, soaking Him in and responding in praise, wonder, love, and delight . . . it would never occur to us whether we were being traditional or contemporary.[3]

I hold the conviction that God doesn't care a diddly whether we're contemporary or traditional in our public worship, it's so completely beside the point!

The number one ingredient for worship is internal: we must know Christ, for no man calls Jesus "Lord" but by the Holy Spirit. And in knowing Christ, we can be led by the Spirit beyond that initial step into the act of worship.

Secondly, I believe that when John 4 says "those who worship Him must worship Him in spirit," it also means in our spirits, in our own right attitude toward God, in our enthusiasm for God. You can't come to worship to survey the situation, to "see how things are going today." No, no! You will never get to God that way. Let me tell you, it's devastating for up-fronters to try to "lead in worship" people who are just careless and casual, greeting their friends, and looking over the situation in an attitude of "bless-me-I-dare-you." It kills the spirit. It dampens hearts. I tell you, it hurts everybody.

Watchman Nee, that great Chinese Christian, wrote:

They cannot be passive in the Body; they dare not merely stand by looking on. For none are so hurtful as onlookers.

Whether or not we take a public part in things is immaterial, we must always be giving life, so that our absence is felt.

We cannot say, "I don't count." We dare not attend meetings merely as passengers, while others do the work.

We are His Body, and members in particular, and it is when all the members fulfill their ministry that the life flows.[4]

And, oh, how God is continually reaching for us in the worship service! If only we understood this. Listen to Moffatt's translation of God's words in Isaiah 65:1:

Ready was I to answer men
  who never asked me,
ready to be found by men
  who never sought me.
I cried out, "Here am I,"
  to folk who never called to me.

But when His Spirit in grace gets to us, and our limited helplessness nevertheless reaches up to Him—oh, my friend—the sparks of love and worship fly.

Think a minute about the story of the Magi in Matthew 2. They were the first Gentiles ever to come to know Christ. Here they came, seeking Him. They didn't have the Scriptures. They knew very little about spiritual things. But they knew enough to make them come a long distance, probably from as far east as Afghanistan, the center of astrology at that time, all the way to the Holy Land. It took them a long time. (Friend, you don't need to know very much to get to God. Just so you know enough to get to Him.)

Matthew 2:1 and 2: "After Jesus was born in Bethlehem in Judea in the days of King Herod, wise men from the east arrived unexpectedly in Jerusalem, saying, 'Where is He who has been born King of the Jews? For we saw His star in the east *and have come to worship Him.*'"

They didn't say they had come to study this unusual situation. They came to worship Him! That touches me. And how they really did it!—"Falling to their knees, they worshiped Him. Then they opened their treasures and presented Him with gifts: gold, frankincense, and myrrh" (Matt. 2:11).

They fell down!

Have you ever prayed actually on your face in humility before God? That's the point of falling down. "I want to be low before God even in my physical position." It would be a good experience for you. Just stretch out on the floor and cry to God.

The Scriptures say that those who know the very most about God—the angels and the archangels in heaven—continually fall down and worship Him (see Rev. 4–5). They are on their faces before God. And John, who had leaned on Jesus' chest and had been His best friend—when John was transported into the world above and saw the risen, glorious Christ, he fell down as dead before Him (see Rev. 1:17). How then can we lean back in church and fold our arms?

These Magi learned to worship right away. Their hearts were sensitive. They fell down and worshiped Him, and then they gave Him gifts—beautiful, expensive gifts. And "they were overjoyed" (Matt. 2:10).

Now let's think about Monday to Saturday. Our Sunday attitudes are so important. This doesn't mean we have to be perfect; we are sinners as we come to worship—all of us, obviously. And God loves us. But we cannot live a double life. Amos puts the finger on this as God speaks through him in Amos 5:21–24: "I hate your show and pretense—your hypocrisy of 'honoring' me with your religious feasts and solemn assemblies. I will not accept your burnt offerings and thank offerings. I will not look at your offerings of peace. Away with your hymns of praise—they are noise to my ears. I will not listen to your music, no matter how lovely it is. I want to see a mighty flood of justice—a torrent of doing good!" (TLB).

God amplifies what He means when He goes on in the eighth chapter: "Listen, you merchants who rob the poor, trampling on the needy; you who long for the Sabbath to end and the religious holidays to be over, so you can get out and start cheating again—using your weighted scales and your under-sized measures; you who make slaves of the poor, buying them for their debt of a piece of silver or a pair of shoes, or selling them your moldy wheat—the Lord, the Pride of Israel, has sworn: 'I won't forget your deeds!'" (vv. 4–7).

Christian, if you really plan to worship, you'll discover your whole life will be changed. What happens? You worship, and God purges your life with holy fire. You come out of a worship service saying, "I'll never do business like that," or "I'll never treat people like that again." You come out into a new way of life. Then back you go into another time of cleansing worship before God with the people of God. Worship burns out sin. When God's people learn real corporate worship, then He is like a consuming fire among them. And the community will say, "I like doing business with the people from that church."

"Worship in spirit," says John 4, but also "worship in ... truth." Two times Jesus says to worship in truth (see vv. 23–24). I believe that means you have to involve your mind in worship.

We live in a very sensuous day. We think we're intellectual, but actually our moods, our feelings, determine much that we think or do.

Years ago automobile tires were advertised by describing the quality of the tire. Today they're often sold by something like showing a girl in a bikini standing by a tire! What's the relationship?

There is none. It's just a sensuous ad. The ad-men hope that by association, when you see that tire, you'll subtly *feel* good, and you'll buy one.

Years ago Folgers Coffee used to be advertised by facts. It was grown in South America; it was roasted in a certain way; it was carefully packaged—and that made it better than other coffees. Now, how does Folgers Coffee advertise? Like this: "Folgers . . . Aaahh!"

Today we can easily get caught using a certain tone of voice—"Jesus . . ." and saying, "Oh-h-h, that's really worshipful!" Not necessarily! Who is this Jesus, Whose name you're repeating? What are your doctrinal facts about Him? What do you mean when you say "Jesus"? You must worship Him in truth! Is He the lovely, risen, exalted, coming again Son of the Living God? We must engage our minds.

A critic once said, "When I go to church, I feel like unscrewing my head and placing it under the seat because in a religious meeting I never have any use for anything above my collar." Now, I'm sorry for him, because if he were at all coming to meet God, he'd have lots to use above his collar. But I think what he's saying is, "I don't like a strictly emotional type of worship in which my mind is not fully engaged."

God is a rational God. He calls on us to come to Him with minds as well as hearts. "Therefore, brothers, by the mercies of God, I urge you to present your bodies [your faculties] as a living sacrifice, holy and pleasing to God; this is your spiritual worship" (Rom. 12:1).

Heaven's population knows all about Christ, and their view of God is true. Their real view of God is full-orbed, and so their enthusiasm is also intelligent and full-orbed! Heaven worships Him best.

Revelation 19 tells of that wonderful scene around the throne of God in heaven: "The twenty-four elders and the four living creatures fell down and worshiped God, who is seated on the throne, saying, 'Amen! Hallelujah!'" (v. 4). (Oh, the great fervor, the heartiness! We need this, too, don't we?) "Then I heard something like the voice of a vast multitude, like the sound of cascading waters, and like the rumbling of loud thunder, saying 'Hallelujah—because our Lord God, the Almighty, has begun to reign! Let us be glad, rejoice, and give Him glory'" (vv. 6–7).

You see, when we know much, we worship and magnify Him much.

Giving your attention to God takes all the concentration you can muster. We evangelicals haven't thought enough about these things. For instance, you need to get ready to worship. Perhaps you should come early, maybe even a half hour, and just sit before God. Or instead of coming in, maybe you need to take a five-minute walk outside, thinking of God, talking to Him. You need to "wind down" so that you can get into worship and "wind up" the right way! You need to learn how to pray and love God before the service.

Friend, you have an appointment with God Almighty, the King of kings, and no cup of coffee, no conversation with any friend should make you late to that appointment. You have an audience with Him. If He sovereignly allows you to have a flat tire on the way, then praise Him as you change it! But pray for yourself as you come in, and pray for others, and pray for those who participate from up front.

Then when you come into church, put blinders on! And help others to wear blinders! Don't move around. Don't be distracting. Don't talk. Slip quietly into church and go to God. Give your whole mind and heart to Him.

At the very first happening of the service, engage your mind. Get with God. Get with the people of God. Sing! Think when you sing, and sing to God. When the choir or special music sings—my, don't read the bulletin! Put that aside; read it when you go home. Let the worship team speak to you for God, and speak to God for you. I beg you in Jesus' name, learn how to worship as others lift you up. The music is merely the vehicle to make the words really come home strongly.

When the Bible is read, do as that hymn says: "Beyond the sacred page, I see Thee, Lord."[5]

When prayer is offered, be with God. He is never dull or boring! Pray for those who pray, that they will prepare and think before they come and be in the Spirit as they pray. It's an awesome thing to lead a company of people in prayer.

During the sermon, take notes. Underline in your Bible. Make some notes to yourself—"This I want to do. . . ." Remember what Paul said to the Corinthian church: "For to those who are perishing the message of the cross is foolishness, but to us who are being saved, it is God's power" (1 Cor. 1:18). The New Testament shows that the sermon is the whole congregation's declaring their faith together. Forsythe, the great preacher, said, "It is the organized hallelujah of the whole church!"

And let me say this: Those leading in worship or preaching—if they're any good—are probably terrified! It's an awesome, draining experience, and it needs the support of much prayer.

At the end of the service, seal it all up and then plan by God's grace to go and *do* the truth.

One final word: Don't be worship-centered; be God-centered! Don't go out of church exclaiming, "Wasn't that some kind of worship," but "Wasn't it great to meet the Lord!" It's no good to be in love with love; you must be in love with your lover.

You want to worship God, to be with Him. Go with your brothers and sisters, with all your hearts, to God together. The words *in spirit and in truth* mean "in the atmosphere of Spirit"—of the Holy Spirit—and "in the atmosphere of truth"—the truth of Christ.

Worship is elevating. It's healing. It's comforting. It's enriching. It's Christ-honoring. It's a growing thing to worship God.

I challenge you to learn how—more and more.

COMMITMENT TWO:

Commit Yourself to the Body of Christ

The little plane jostled through air pockets high over South American mountain peaks, and four of us looked in each other's eyes: Cliff, Carl, my wife Anne, and me. Then we prayed together above the roar of the motor.

"Lord, here we are. You're sending us to minister to these Wycliffe missionaries of Colombia and Panama. We know almost none of them, but we believe in Your strategy. You're going to bring us together for a reason. . . ."

I'd been asked to be speaker at the annual business and inspiration get-together of this Wycliffe branch, but because of Commitment Number Two, we'd been learning at Lake Avenue Church not to move in solo motions. We ministered in teams. We made decisions with the brothers and sisters. We "got sent" or we didn't "go."

So I'd answered Wycliffe, as I do all speaking invitations, "Look, I'll come if I can bring a team. From somewhere God will scare up the money."

"A-OK" came the answer, and we prayed as the Spirit chose Anne (her plane fare was offered out of the blue), and Cliff and

Carl, a school principal and a dentist, who each arranged to be released from his work.

The four of us already knew and loved each other well. But as usual, in preparation God ground us by mortar and pestle until we were one stuff.

Wasn't the same always true with Paul and his teams? Of Barnabas, Silas, Timothy, Titus, etc., Paul wrote, "For we have the same Holy Spirit, and walk in each other's steps, doing things the same way" (2 Cor. 12:18 TLB).

So the little plane descended into Loma Linda, a clearing in the jungle—"Honda City," Carl named it. We four met once a day to report, pray, plan, laugh, cry, and beseech God. Otherwise we scattered, multiplying ourselves: four mouths with one message.

In the meetings any or all of us might speak. We were the Body at work. Commitment Number Two in three dimensions.

Then we discovered what we were there for. Dear missionaries! How wonderful they were.

Obviously they were committed to Number One—God—or they would never have trained to become highly skilled linguists, turning their backs on well-paying American jobs to translate the Bible from unknown tongues.

Obviously they were committed to Number Three—their work—or they would never have slogged their way to some of the world's most primitive areas to spend years putting strange grunts and groans on paper.

But commitment to the Body? They had jumped from One to Three, and they were lonely even in their togetherness.

We told them how we were learning to do it in the Company of the Committed: In small groups—"I'm responsible for you, and you're responsible for me. . . . Everything I have is yours; use me. . . . I'll agonize over your kids, and you agonize over mine. . . . Teach me what you know in the Word, and I'll teach you what I know. . . . Here's where I'm weak; hold me accountable, and pray me to strength. . . . Let's learn together to worship God. . . ."

For these very committed, zealous, work-oriented accomplishers, the cry was, "How do I have time for this? I can hardly get my work done now."

Four work-pressed Pasadenans freshly out of the Great Southern California Pace said, "Then you postpone your goals. The Body comes first—Priority Two!—your wife, your children, your lonely neighbor, your hurting friend."

On the eighth day, Thursday morning at an eight o'clock meeting, the Wycliffe branch of Colombia-Panama melted into a working part of the Body of Christ. (Somebody chuckled afterward, "I always thought revival could only happen at night!")

Christians expressed their love for each other. They apologized for past hurts. Tears and laughter ebbed and flowed as they poured out what they'd been holding inside for a long time. They prayed for each other on the spot. Very real and human fears of the jungle melted away. Genuine compassion and love for the Indian tribes was kindled. Believers sought out believers and automatically became small groups.

I heard the other day of a tape from one of them, reporting eighteen months later how life-changing that week was for him.

Christian, the priorities cannot be Three, One. They can't be One, Three. They've got to be One, Two, Three.

In that order.

chapter five
PUT IT TOGETHER WITH OTHER BELIEVERS

A kid I know who went off to college for the first time wrote, "Mom, I'm so lonesome. Deep down inside I feel so unsure of myself."

An older friend said to me recently, "I've known a sense of aloneness all my life, but never more keenly than now. My children are nice to me. I know they love me. But I'm a problem to them. I'd like to talk to them, share my heart, but when I try, I can see that they don't understand."

We all know loneliness. Christ comes to deal with this sense of aloneness by bringing us into fellowship with Him and His church. Many an older Christian, and many a younger one coming out of non-Christian backgrounds, have said to me, "You know, I feel closer to people of my church than I feel to my own family. Here they truly understand me."

The greatest resource that you and I have is the presence of Jesus Christ Himself. The second most precious possession is the fellowship of God's people.

I want you to look at three basic Scriptures that have to do with fellowship—relationships in the family of God. One is from Matthew; one, from Malachi; one, from Romans.

Matthew speaks of the promised presence of Christ among His people. Malachi speaks of the attitude of God toward those who gather together to worship Him. And in Romans, Paul gives the spiritual ingredients of Christian friendship and fellowship.

So let's go to these. Matthew 18:20 records words spoken by Jesus: "For where two or three are gathered together in My name, I am there among them."

The context of Matthew 18 says that He gives power and authority to the gathered people of God. Christ loves the gathering of those who love Him. Even the smallest number is important to Him. He knows, you see, the tragedy, danger, and inadequacy of spiritual aloneness. He knows the failure of the Christian who lives in voluntary solitary confinement. To be alone (unless it is ordained of God, when someone is thrust into this because of some special situation)—to choose to be alone—is to invite sure failure.

Remember in the Old Testament when the Jews were instructed by Moses' law to gather together several times a year. They came from far and near, from all over, to Jerusalem to be together. Sometimes they came to eat for a whole week; sometimes to weep together; sometimes to rejoice in all that God had done; sometimes to repent. But these huge gatherings of God's people were so important because by their gathering together, God knew that they would maintain their identity as His chosen people. "Where two or three are gathered together in My name, I am there."

The psalmist talks about the gathering of Israel. David says, "We walked with the throng at the house of God" (Ps. 55:14). Isn't that beautiful? That's why Hebrews says, "Let us . . . not [be] staying away from meetings, as some habitually do, but [let us be] encouraging each other, and all the more as you see the day [of Christ's return] drawing near" (Heb. 10:24–25).

But Sunday church services, wonderful as they are, aren't enough. Catch the flavor of the lifestyle of the early Christians. Acts 2:44–46 tells how they met together constantly, daily—in two ways: they worshiped together regularly in the temple, everybody all at once; and they broke bread together daily in small groups in each other's homes.

Not either/or, my friend, but both. The church service will be cold if you come together as strangers. (And believe me, I mean strangers who have known each other for years!) But when you've been together constantly in small groups—studying, praying, confessing your needs, holding each other accountable, lifting each other up—then you'll be drawn together on Sunday into the magnetic field of Holy Spirit-filled love and praise!

Back again to these small groups. Jesus says, "Where two or three are gathered together _in My name_. . . ." The basis of our special friendships is the name of Christ. We are people of the Name. Someone said, "Every man is like the company he keeps." Or, "Tell me your company, and I will tell you what you are." Thomas Carlyle said, "Show me the man you honor, and by that, better than any other, I know what kind of a man you are." Wise Solomon writes in Proverbs 13:20,

> He who walks with the wise grows wise,
>> but a companion of fools suffers harm.

Ultimately, you choose your own friends. Be sure to choose them carefully. They're your responsibility! And if your friendships are meaningfully, purposefully in Christ, you should find in these deep gatherings together that something wonderful happens to you. You become an imitator of the people you're with.

We're all like that white "boring" shell that's found at the beach. If it attaches itself to a brown rock, it becomes brown; or a red rock, it becomes red. More awesome yet with us believers, as Christ is among us, we all become more and more like Him.

Now turn to Malachi 3:16. Christ not only promises to meet with those who meet with others in His name, but also He records what we talk about when we meet together! This is amazing, sobering. "Then those who feared the LORD spoke with one another; the LORD heeded and heard them, and a book of remembrance was written before him of those who feared the LORD and thought on his name" (RSV).

Note that the King James Version says "spake often one to another," but I think that weakens it a bit. The word *often* was not in the original. This was not a "now again, then again" happening; this was a way of life! His people were continually talking about God together.

This talking together has to be a structured thing. Otherwise, even though our intentions are good, our lives are too cluttered and it gets crowded out.

My wife, Anne, wears a bracelet given to her by her three special Christian sisters. It has three charms on it, each one engraved with a name and a particular Bible verse. Let me describe to you how these four "spoke with one another" for one particular twelve-month period. Every Tuesday and Thursday morning, each phoned each of the other three. Each sister knew she was to be ready with something to share from the Scriptures—something fresh since the last telephone call. Then the last few days would be reviewed. Needs would be prayed for over the telephone. Praise would be offered for successes. The days' schedules until next contact time would be projected and prayed over. Then every other Wednesday noon, the four met for lunch, and this meeting was primarily for praise, adoration, and worship. In the days of my pastoring Lake Avenue Church, something like this kind of structured "speaking together" in small groups was duplicated hundreds of times over each week.

Notice Malachi says that God "heeded" them. He noticed them right away. He bent over and listened, and He wrote down what they said. God watches carefully that we fulfill our human responsibility of sharing our hearts with some of His other people. God's attitude toward fellowship is that wherever there is fellowship, He comes!

Of course, why wouldn't this be true? Our God is a togetherness God. He is Father, Son, and Holy Spirit. He's not a single unit, an isolated loner. Our God is *in Himself* fellowship, and we who are made in His image were not made to be loners—to make our decisions all by ourselves, to hoard our resources for ourselves, to turn inward, to be solitary figures among other solitary figures.

The word *fellowship* is an interesting one. It comes from an Anglo-Saxon word that is really "fee"-lowship. The word *fee* meant cow, and cows in those days were a man's wealth! (We still use the word *fee* today for a charge for payment of money.)

So when people really trusted each other, they established a joint bank account—they put their cows together. The walls were broken down, the fences removed; they could put their cows together. They'd say, "I want to have fellowship with you. I trust you."

This is how God calls us together. I have a deep suspicion that we twenty-first-century believers have much to learn from the early Christians' pooling their funds. We haven't even begun to take seriously yet what deep fellowship can mean.

Billy Graham, when asked what he would do if he pastored a church today, said this: "I think one of the first things I would do would be to get a small group of eight or ten or twelve men around me who would meet a few hours a week and pay the price! It would cost them something in time and effort. I would share with them everything I have, over a period of a couple years. Then I would actually have twelve ministers among the laymen, who in turn could take eight or ten or twelve more and teach them."[1]

Christ Himself has set the pattern. He spent most of His time with twelve—with eternal results. He called the Twelve that they might be with Him. He worked with them, trained them and loved them, and He let them train each other. There was a cross-current of the work of God's Spirit as these disciples were together.

Discipling is as crucial a need as there is among believers today. Every Christian needs an older Christian he's learning from and a younger Christian he's teaching. It's the function of the whole Body to do this.

Believer, whom do you know who could disciple you? Pray over it, and then go ask if he feels led to take you on. Be willing to pay the price of submission. But don't forget that Ephesians 5 says submission is required of *all* of us, as we're filled with the Holy Spirit.

And then, whom should you disciple? Don't just pour your life into anybody. If they're too involved in this world, they'll probably always just follow Jesus afar off. But look for these qualifications:

• Heart
• Teachability
• Availability

This is obedience to the last command Christ ever gave us: "Go and make disciples of all nations, . . . teaching them to obey everything I have commanded you" (Matt. 28:19–20 NIV).

This is gutsy, biblical Christianity!

Paul did this. He never went out alone. You notice it's usually Paul with Timothy, or with Timothy and Silas, writing to the churches. Turn to the last part of Romans and you see it isn't just Paul alone: "Timothy, my co-worker . . . greet[s] you" (16:21). He travels with a band of men, and he's committed to men who are committed to him. Why? Because Timothy is one of his travelers, one of those who is with him, one of the "cell group," a partner in the gospel. Paul also says, "Lucius, Jason, and Sosipater, my fellow countrymen, greet you. I Tertius [their secretary] . . . greet you" (vv. 21–22). And then Romans 16:23 says, "Gaius, who is host to me and to the whole church, greets you." Paul never flew solo!

God works great things in His gathered people.

Many years ago there were a few men who were meeting for prayer at Williams College in Massachusetts. One day as they were meeting, praying about world needs, a storm came up, and they took refuge under the overhanging shelf of a haystack. There under that haystack, God met them in such a great way that they began what we know today as the modern missionary movement. Those men fanned out all over the world. It was God meeting them as they were committed to each other and to the gospel together, and God guided and directed them from that haystack around the globe.

A former priest of Trinity Episcopal Church on Wall Street in New York once wrote: "It is a growing conviction of mine that no parish can fulfill its true function unless there is at the very center of its leadership life, a small community of quietly fanatic, changed and truly converted Christians. The trouble with most parishes is that nobody, including the rector, is really greatly changed; but even where there is a devoted, self-sacrificing priest at the heart of the fellowship, not much will happen until there is a community of changed men and women."[2]

This happens as men and women draw their hearts together in small groups for prayer, for study of the Word, and for communion and fellowship together.

In Romans, Paul gives the spiritual ingredients of Christian friendship and fellowship. *First,* he tells us to make our fellowships broad. Don't just gather people around you who think as you think. Romans 15:1–3 says, "We who are strong have an obligation to bear the weaknesses of those without strength, and not to please ourselves. Each one of us must please his neighbor for his good, in order to build him up. For even the Messiah did not please Himself."

In your friendships, include weak people. You may ask, "Who are the weak?" Look at chapter 14, verses 1 and 2: "Accept anyone who is weak in faith, but don't argue about doubtful issues. One person believes he may eat anything, but *one who is weak eats only vegetables.*"

The weak person is the legalist, the one who gets his security out of not doing this and doing that. Paul says in the next verses, "Now, don't despise this person. Receive him. Love him. Don't be narrow and restricted in your fellowship *because you feel he might be.*"

Verse 19 of chapter 14: "We must pursue what promotes peace and what builds up one another." Our fellowship can be rich in differences, proving that none other than the Holy Spirit is the glue that holds us tightly together!

Secondly, make your fellowships genuine. Romans 15:7 says: "Accept one another, just as the Messiah also accepted [received] you, to the glory of God."

How did Christ accept or receive you? Well, He received you with your hang-ups and your sins and your troubles and your immaturity. He received you just as you were. And in the same way, we're to come to each other just as we are. We sing a hymn,

> Just as I am
> Without one plea,
> But that Thy blood
> Was shed for me; . . .
> Lamb of God, I come.

Unless we welcome each other just as we are, there will be no place for genuine fellowship. The Word breaks down isolation, and receiving and welcoming one another breaks down barriers.

Proverbs 27:19 says, "As in water face answereth to face, so the heart of man to man" (KJV). This is the way we are to be together—open, reflecting to each other what we really are.

James tells you to confess your faults to each other so that you may be healed (see James 5:16). This is possible where people have been working closely together, and they finally find that they can be absolutely open because they're loved. I don't think there ought to be brutal frankness, where you "mow everybody down" because you say you're being honest. I don't want any kind of fellowship like that. I need to be handled tenderly, and so do you.

Even when we've come to church for years, we can be unknown and lonely. If you never share with anyone your real self, your real thoughts, your real longings—that, my friend, is aloneness. God wants to break that down and bring you into Christian fellowship where you're received.

A Congregational minister came to Lake Avenue Church's Wednesday evening prayer meeting once when I was pastor. We often broke into small groups to pray. The people in his group were introducing each other. He said, "I'm an engineer. I'm out here with my company, but on weekends I preach. I've got some concerns, and I'd like you to pray for them." That man could come to a fellowship of Pasadena Christians and just be himself! We all joined with him and his life and his loves and his purposes, and there was fellowship. And he prayed for us and our needs. He could go back to Wisconsin feeling truly received by Christians in Pasadena. "Carry one another's burdens," says Galatians 6:2, "in this way you will fulfill the law of Christ."

Make your fellowships broad; make them genuine.

Thirdly, the Scripture tells you to make your fellowships useful, to reach out and have ministries together. It's not just so that you'll feel good. You and others must be bound together in purpose. There's a triangle of strategy here: for God, for helping each other, and then for outward ministry. You have to have something that's really important. Fellowship isn't two people looking at each other; it's two people looking away together at something else—at Christ and His purposes.

"[Stand] firm in one spirit, with one mind," says Paul, "working side by side for the faith of the gospel" (Phil. 1:27). That's real Christian fellowship and comradeship, and it's so appealing. It's so good, and the world can't possibly deny this.

One evening a group of men were meeting in downtown New York City. They had met for some time together, and they had wonderful fellowship, sharing the Word of God and sharing their hearts' concerns.

A stranger came in. Each thought that someone else had invited him. The man just sat in and listened as they shared about their frustrations and their needs, and as they enjoyed sharing the gospel and loving Christ and reading the Word together.

Finally they asked this fellow who he was. He said, "My name is Paul. As long as you have been honest, I'll be honest. I'm a dope addict. I came here to rob you to get a fix. But I think I've found something better."

Yes, fellowship is something infinitely better!

My Christian friend, how are you doing?

chapter six
HAVE A CLOSE FRIEND

*W*hen a woman knits, she uses two needles—one in her right hand and one in her left. As she knits, two pieces of yarn, the left and the right, come together to become one solid fabric.

First Samuel 18:1 says that "the soul of Jonathan was knit with the soul of David, and Jonathan loved him as his own soul" (KJV).

You were made to so knit your life with others, that together you weave a beautiful fabric for the glory of God.

Let me share my heart with you about friendships—friendships that last forever. Not friendliness; everyone should be friendly to everyone else. But I'm talking about establishing selective, godly friendships. Let's look at the story of Jonathan and David, how their friendship began, how it developed, and how it continued.

Start with 1 Samuel 14 and meet Jonathan. Goliath had begun coming down and challenging the Israelites for battle between himself and whomever they might choose. Young, unknown David defeated Goliath and won the day—and won Jonathan's admiration. But a few weeks before that, Jonathan had had quite a day all by himself.

The Philistines were making raids on the Israelites. They were strong, they were threatening, and the whole safety of Israel was at stake. Every able Israelite was out in the hills and valleys in defense—even the king's son, Jonathan: "Jonathan said to the young man who bore his armor, 'Come, let us go over to the garrison of these uncircumcised; it may be that the LORD will work for us; for nothing can hinder the LORD from saving by many or by few'" (1 Sam. 14:6 RSV).

Isn't that great? Jonathan says to his armor-bearer, "Naturally the Lord is going to win the battle, whether by many or by few. Hey, just for fun, let's see if He does it by few—like two?"

Here we see several exciting things about Jonathan: of course, his spirit—that he was bold for God, full of faith and courage—but also that before he ever met David, he knew how to make deep friendships. Between him and his armor-bearer there was commitment of heart to heart: "And his armor-bearer said to him, 'Do all that your mind inclines to; behold, I am with you, as is your mind so is mine'" (v. 7). "Jonathan," he says, "I'm yours. You say the word and we'll go."

These two young believers were absolutely counting on God to use them. And He did: "*And [the Philistines] fell before Jonathan*" (v. 13)!

As a result, all Israel loved Jonathan; and when there came a problem between Jonathan and his father, Saul, all the people rose up and said, "Don't touch a hair of Jonathan's head" (see v. 45). He was a real hero.

Such a man as Jonathan—why do you suppose he then allowed Goliath to come up those forty days and taunt Israel? Having gone through such experiences, why would he let one man shake the cage of Israel so badly? I don't really know, and I suppose nobody does, because we're not told. But maybe Jonathan came back after this tremendous rout of the enemy, and he saw all those weak-kneed, unbelieving people, and he saw his father the king slipping back into his old depressions, disobeying God and losing control of the people—and Jonathan might have said, "What's the use? Nobody cares."

But when he saw David walk out of that valley with Goliath's head in his hand—David, just a shepherd boy, a slight lad, younger than Jonathan himself—I can imagine that a man with a heart like Jonathan's said, "How about that? How about that? There's my man! What a man!" Or something like that. Jonathan loved manliness, and David was a manly young man.

I don't know about you, but I desperately need men around me who are giant-killers. I have an innate tendency to fear; I need fearless, godly men. The story of many a Christian is that he starts warm with God—"Take it all, Lord. You can have anything I have." As a result God blesses him and pretty soon he "has it made." Then he wants to "keep it made" and protect himself, and he no longer gets out where he's depending wholly on God. I fear this! Oh, how I fear this.

We simply have to be out on the cutting edge, my friend, or there's enough sin in every one of us that after awhile we'll just be "zeros." That's why a godly friend or two is utterly essential. They must be friends who are courageous enough to exhort and rebuke us, as well as encourage us.

With all our emphasis these days on the Body, I think we have hardly even discovered the possibility of what a Spirit-given, committed friend can do in our lives.

A young fellow said to me recently, "I don't know whether my brothers in my group are really committed to me or not. A month ago I shared with them three goals I'd like to reach: to establish a consistent daily quiet time, to stick to a diet that will take off fifteen pounds, and to adhere rigidly to a new budget that will discipline my wife and me not to overspend."

He looked at me earnestly. "I can't make it without these guys. But since I told them about these goals four weeks ago, not one of them has asked me how I'm doing. Not one has checked up on me."

"Tell them!" I said. "They're responsible for you! If they've committed their hearts to you, your failure is their failure. You're all in this together."

The next morning was their weekly breakfast together, and my young friend laid it on the table. "Do you guys love me, or don't you? Do you care, or not?"

I saw him again soon afterward. He grinned, "Man, those guys were smitten. Almost every day since, somebody's called me—hey, you sticking to your diet? You had your quiet time yet today? No impulse buying, Buddy. . . ."

There was great confidence in his eyes. "I'll make it," he said. My answer was, "Their need to keep responsible for you is just as great as your need to keep accountable to them."

I want you to see how this friendship of Jonathan and David developed. Chapter 18 says that "the soul of Jonathan was knit to the soul of David, and Jonathan loved him as his own soul." The knitting process calls for skill and care. If we're going to have friendships in which our hearts are knit together with others, we must carefully select people God gives us who will join their hearts with ours.

There are many people I'd love to have my heart knit together with, but knitting takes time. So the point is to look for those people whom because of circumstances I'm naturally thrown in with. God says to us, by the very example of Jonathan and David, "Listen, become deep friends with someone, or with two, three, or four."

Someone may ask, "How many can it be?" I don't know what your capacity for loving is. Paul knit his heart together with many people. In Colossians 2 he prayed that Christians' hearts might be knit together in love (v. 2) because he had experienced this. Everywhere Paul went he had a young brother with him. As he wrote to this church and that place, he told how dearly he loved his guys: how Epaphroditus was willing to lay down his life for him (see Phil. 2:25–27), and how Timothy encouraged him in the Lord (2 Tim. 1:3–5). The Body of Christ today must be knit together in the same way.

Wherever you are, Christian, because of your place in life, you can be close to some other believer. Have you someone that your heart is knit to? Are there several to whom you've so committed yourself that you are theirs and they are yours?

Shakespeare's Hamlet says of special friends, "Grapple them to thy soul with hoops of steel!"

Jesus, in the days of His flesh, had three very special friends. Then He had the Twelve—very close. He poured His time into them. Then He had the seventy whom He trained and sent forth. Then there were the hundred and twenty. He loved them all alike, in a sense. Yet He was particularly woven into the fabric of the lives of some who were very special.

Today, of course, Jesus is risen, ascended, and is no longer limited physically or geographically. Now He can say to each one of us, "I will be with you. I will never leave you nor forsake you." The miracle of the resurrected, omnipresent One is that He is knit to us as the closest Friend of all. As bone is knit to bone, so is the Head perfectly fused to the Body.

But the way we learn to express our love for the Head is the way we learn to express our love for somebody who is flesh and blood—with all the nitty-gritty working-out of love that that involves!

David and Jonathan's friendship was not just a pink cloud of emotion. It began with a verbal agreement: "Then Jonathan made a covenant with David, because he loved him as his own soul. And Jonathan stripped himself of the robe that was upon him, and gave it to David, and his armor, and even his sword and his bow and his girdle" (1 Sam. 18:3–4 RSV).

This was a tremendously symbolic thing. Remember that Jonathan was heir apparent to the throne—he was Saul's son. David was his subject. But Jonathan loved him so, he took off his special robe and gave it to David. And he took off the belt in which he

had his wealth, and he gave that to David. In this way he was saying, "All I have is yours, David. Everything I have."

Listen, have you ever said that to anybody? No? Then you
haven't lived. You need to say to somebody, "Everything I have is
yours." It's easy to be a loner, to protect yourself for yourself. There
are lots of evangelical loners! They really do love Jesus, but they
don't love His church too much. That's incongruous, and it's sin.
Real fellowship calls for gutsy commitment.

Christ Himself initiates this kind of friendship. He says to you,
"Everything I have is yours. All My righteousness I give to you."
The "riches of his glory" by Christ Jesus are yours. And He says,
"Now, you give Me everything of yours in return." You say, "All
right, Lord, I give You my sins, I give You my failures, I give You
my inabilities." And He says, "Fine, fine! That's a deal." Then He
gives you forgiveness, constant love, friendship. Beautiful!

When we've done that, we're ready for godly friendships with
each other. How we Christians of today need to learn the fullness
of the Christian life! This isn't *all* the Christian life, but it is a very
important part—to strip ourselves for each other, my friend. To
strip ourselves.

We don't know this yet. God is working to teach us. I was meeting weekly with a small group of seminary students. What quality
young men! And how they had given their hearts to each other!

But one afternoon as we met together, one of them was totally
discouraged. "I just can't make it financially, with Joanie and the
baby," he said. "I've got to drop out of seminary."

One of the other fellow's eyes filled with tears. "Ted," he said
(I'm using fictitious names), "I never want to hear you say that
again. You're a good student, and obviously God wants you to fin-
ish. As long as you're in school, whenever you need money, I'll supply it. Just let me know. I don't ever again want to hear you talk of
quitting because of finances."

You're probably thinking this fellow had money. He didn't.
He was also going through seminary with a wife and baby, and he

was as poor as Ted. He just happened to have more faith in that particular area. It was a holy moment.

I never heard whether Ted ever asked Frank for money. I only know that both Ted and Frank knew the offer was absolutely valid. And I know that Ted finished seminary—on schedule, with a good academic record.

There's an exquisite scene in 1 Samuel 20:42. Look at it. Remember that David had to hide from King Saul because Saul was so jealous. And now Jonathan and David are meeting alone: "Then Jonathan said to David, 'Go in peace, forasmuch as we have sworn both of us in the name of the LORD . . . .'" (RSV).

What did they swear to each other? Listen: "The LORD shall be between me and you." They were bound together in God. The Lord was the cohesive factor. I want you to see how deep and long-standing their friendship was to be. Jonathan continues: "And [the Lord shall be] between my descendants and your descendants, for ever."

That's saying, "I will love your kids; and my kids will love your kids; and my kids' kids are going to love your kids' kids!" I can hardly imagine anything more marvelous than this. How deep their friendship was to go! They not only bound their lives together, but they bound their children's lives together, and their children's children's lives after that.

In 1 Samuel 23 we see the last time these two friends will ever meet. They don't know it, but very soon Jonathan is going to be killed in battle: "David was afraid because Saul had come out to seek his life. David was in the Wilderness of Ziph at Horesh. And Jonathan, Saul's son, rose, and went to David at Horesh, and strengthened his hand in God" (vv. 15–16 RSV).

"David was afraid." This is where a friend must come in. Jonathan finds him and says, "Oh, David, don't ever forget that God has anointed you to be king. David, take heart!" And he "strengthened his hand in God."

"He said to him, 'Fear not; for the hand of Saul my father shall not find you; you shall be king over Israel, and I shall be next to you; Saul my father also knows this'" (v. 17). What an amazing thing for Jonathan to say—Jonathan, physically next in line to the throne! "David, my joy is that you will be the king, and if I can just stand next to you, that will be enough."

Friend, do you know how to support your friend in God? Wife, do you ever strengthen your husband's hand in God? Husband, do you ever strengthen your wife in God? Or you men whose hearts are bound together, do you strengthen each other with the Word of God and with encouragement? Do you know how to give this?

"You know [Timothy's] proven character," wrote Paul, "because he has served with me in the gospel ministry like a son with a father" (Phil. 2:22).

Some of us men were sitting around a conference table at our church. What had begun as a committee had become a band of men. God had knit our hearts together. And now we were pledging ourselves to one another. None of us will ever forget it. One was discouraged—dear, dear friend. He said, "I don't know if I can commit myself to you. I'm so discouraged; I feel so weak; I don't have anything to offer to you guys." And one of the other men said, "All right, this is the time for us to pour our lives into you. There'll come a time later when you can strengthen us."

Jonathan said to David, "I'm stronger now, but soon you will be. You'll be king, and I shall just stand by your side." Gladly Jonathan hands over all the glory of position to David. What wonderful selflessness! "I shall be next to you."

I wonder if David, after Jonathan died, ever thought, *Oh, Jonathan, man I loved, I feel you next to me. In a different way than you thought, Jonathan, you'll always be next to me!*

Hebrews 12:1 tells about the "large cloud of witnesses surrounding us." The testimony of all those saints through the years continually surrounds us and encourages us: "Stand firm! Believe God."

Thank You, Lord.

I want my memory to linger with somebody. I want to stand by somebody when I'm gone.

Even after death, the friendship between Jonathan and David continued—unbroken. The last chapter of 1 Samuel states, "Now the Philistines fought against Israel; the Israelites fled before them, and many fell slain on Mount Gilboa. The Philistines pressed hard after Saul and his sons, and they killed . . . Jonathan" (1 Sam. 31:1–2).

Second Samuel 1:11–12 tells what happens when David hears about it: "David took hold of his clothes, and rent them; and so did all the men who were with him; and they mourned and wept and fasted until evening for Saul and for Jonathan his son and for the people of the LORD and for the house of Israel, because they had fallen by the sword" (RSV).

And then verse 17: "And David lamented with this lamentation over Saul and Jonathan. . . ."

"Saul and Jonathan!" How beautiful for David to speak so kindly of Saul, who had haunted him and threatened him all his life! David's word was "Touch not the Lord's anointed" (see 1 Chron. 16:22; 1 Sam. 24:10). He was a man who just wouldn't speak evil of another. Look at the magnanimous spirit of David: "Saul and Jonathan," he sings, "beloved and lovely! In life and in death they were not divided" (2 Sam. 1:23 RSV).

How the mighty have fallen in battle!

Jonathan lies slain on your heights.

I grieve for you, Jonathan my brother;
    you were very dear to me.
Your love for me was wonderful,
    more wonderful than that of women.
How the mighty have fallen! (vv. 25–27)

Friend, do you have a loving circle of friends with whom, when they live, you live; and when they die, in a sense, you die? Do you have friends who will love you and your children and your children's children? If you don't have anyone like that, step out by faith. Live a little dangerously, and give your heart away. Find someone who will be a godly friend to you, who will strengthen your hand in God. I plead with you for this.

If the only thing you can talk about is where you went to dinner last or what your golf score is—those things are good to talk about once in awhile—you've got to get deeper than that. Sometimes you've got to get to the soul! You and God and that person must link your hearts and arms together and say, "We're going to go together. We love each other, and we're going to pray each other through hard times and good times, and lift each other up."

About 1638, the Old Scotch Covenanters in Edinburgh went out in a churchyard and drew up a covenant together. They vowed that they would "hang together," and they signed the covenant with the blood of their own veins. That was the beginning of a powerful movement of God in human history.

How true was David to his pledge of commitment? Look at 2 Samuel 4:4: "Jonathan, the son of Saul, had a son who was crippled in his feet. He was five years old when the news about Saul and Jonathan came from Jezreel; and his nurse took him up, and fled; and, as she fled in her haste, he fell, and became lame. And his name was Mephibosheth" (RSV).

In 5:12 we read: "And David perceived that the LORD had established him king over Israel, and that he had exalted his kingdom for the sake of his people Israel" (RSV). David had "arrived." He "had it made." Outwardly, he needed no one.

All right, David, how about your pledge to Jonathan about his children? How good is your word?

You remember in the beautiful movie *Song of Norway* Edvard Grieg's struggle to succeed as a composer. His friend had poured his life into him. When the friend was dying, he sent word to Edvard, "Come see me." But Edvard had become a big hero, and there were concerts, receptions. He never made it. What a heartbreak! I don't know about you, but I wept.

What about David, now so successful, the darling of the people? "And David said, 'Is there still any one left of the house of Saul, that I may show him kindness for Jonathan's sake?'" (2 Sam. 9:1 RSV). Hooray! Good for you, David!

"Mephibosheth the son of Jonathan, son of Saul, came to David, and fell on his face and did obeisance. . . . And David said to him, 'Do not fear; for I will show you kindness for the sake of your father Jonathan, and I will restore to you all the land of Saul your father; and you shall eat at my table always'" (2 Sam. 9:6–7 RSV).

At one time Chile and Argentina were about to go to battle. But they came to their senses and made a pact, a covenant of peace. To commemorate that covenant, they erected a huge statue called "The Christ of the Andes." At the bottom of that statue these words are inscribed:

Sooner shall these mountains crumble to dust,
than Chile and Argentina shall break the peace they
have sworn at the feet of the Redeemer.

I speak to you in the name of Christ, Who said, "I do not call you slaves anymore, because a slave doesn't know what his master is doing. I have called you friends" (John 15:15).

Jesus says, "I am willing to expose My heart to you."

Will you, too, expose your heart?

With one friend, or several, make a pact at the feet of the Redeemer![1]

chapter seven

FIND YOUR
SPIRITUAL GIFT

You look around a church in wonder. It's an organization of volunteers; almost nobody's paid. And yet every Sunday there's a vase of beautifully arranged flowers by the pulpit. Somebody who cooks keeps turning out those church dinners. Helpful people usher, and teachers teach. . . .

The phenomenon of the gifts of the Holy Spirit exploded after the resurrection of Christ out of the grave and His glorious ascension into heaven. Do you realize that the resurrection and the gifts of the Spirit are linked? After Christ rose, these tremendous gifts were given to believers. This was prophesied in Psalm 68:18: "Thou hast ascended on high, thou hast led captivity captive: thou hast received gifts for men; yea, for the rebellious also, that the LORD God might dwell among them" (KJV).

When Paul wrote in Ephesians 4 about Christ's resurrection and the subsequent gifts of the Spirit, he quoted this very verse from Psalm 68.

Note that all God's people were to receive gifts, even the

rebellious ones. Gifts are not prizes or rewards, given only to deserving Christians.

The point is that first Christ came out of the grave and assumed His position as head of the Church. Then the Holy Spirit was released upon the world. And only then, a man who was a former fisherman became a tremendous evangelist—preaching with such power that after one message, three thousand confessed the Lord. And a tax collector who was formerly just a scheming little man soon became large in his understanding, writing one of the greatest pieces of literature of all time—the Gospel of Matthew. And we could go on.

In Peter's sermon in Acts 2, he explains the sudden coming of these gifts: "God has resurrected this Jesus. We are all witnesses of this. Therefore, since He has been exalted to the right hand of God and has received from the Father the promised Holy Spirit, He has poured out what you both see and hear" (vv. 32–33).

At Pentecost the risen Christ was glorified among His people. The mighty acts of God were proclaimed in the various languages of the people—a supernatural thing. Evangelism and teaching were suddenly abundant among the people. And whoosh! The church began to operate with its many-sided gifts.

Paul says in 1 Corinthians 12:1, "Now about spiritual gifts, brothers, I do not want you to be ignorant" (NIV). And then he goes on to show us how we are all alike, and how we are all different.

Verses 1 to 3 tell how we're alike in the Spirit. Paul says, "You know how, when you were pagans"—(and the pagans had their vast systems of witchcraft, their trances, their dreams, their visions)—"*you were led to dumb idols—being led astray.*" Paul says that there was a force behind the scenes driving them to all kinds of evil—a demonic power. Then he says, "Therefore I am informing you that no one speaking by the Spirit of God says, 'Jesus is cursed,' and no one can say, 'Jesus is Lord,'"—(That's what you would call the irreducible statement of Christian faith: "Jesus is Lord")—"except by the Holy Spirit."

Today great, exciting hosts of us around the world are saying without any hesitation, "Jesus is Lord!"

No one calls Jesus cursed by the Spirit of God. Another power altogether says that. When some oath that curses Christ comes out of a person's mouth, an evil power is behind it.

Notice that word *same*—"same Spirit"—in verses 4, 8, and 9. We have one life-power in us all. There's a beautiful area north of Los Angeles called Thousand Oaks, and it does seem that there must be a thousand oak trees out on the lovely hillsides of that community. Each of the thousand oaks is different, and yet there is one oak-life that pulsates through each of those trees.

Each human body is unified because it is possessed and occupied by one person. So the Body of Christ is unified because it is possessed and occupied by God Himself.

When you came to Christ, the Holy Spirit gave you a supernatural specialty, just for you. It doesn't mean that other people may not have that—there may be many who do—but He has given you a specialty to make your Christian life fulfilled and meaningful. It isn't spooky, my friend; it's practical.

And He's left no one out! Verse 11 says, "But one and the same Spirit is active in all these, distributing to *each one* as He wills."

"As *He* wills." You are no more left to choose your gift, or your gifts, than you are left to choose the color of your eyes. It is just *as He wills.* I'm glad.

We are all alike in three ways: we've been influenced by the Spirit; we have been given gifts by the Spirit; and we have been baptized by the Spirit into the Body of Christ.

Verse 13 says: "For we were all baptized by one Spirit into one body—whether Jews or Greeks, whether slaves or free—and we were all made to drink of one Spirit."

Now, this baptism has nothing to do with water, any more than the baptism Jesus talked about when He asked, "Are you willing to be baptized with the baptism I am going to be baptized with?" (see Mark 10:38). These men had already been baptized with water. Jesus was talking about the cross. Baptism does not always imply water.

The basic meaning of the word *baptism* is "to identify with." He is saying here that we are all identified by the Holy Spirit into the Body of Christ—placed into the Body of Christ.

This phrase *baptize with the Holy Spirit* is mentioned seven times in the New Testament. John the Baptist said, "I baptize with water; He will baptize with the Holy Spirit"—speaking of Christ. This saying is quoted in Matthew, Mark, Luke, and John (see Matt. 3:11; Mark 1:8; Luke 3:16–17; John 1:26, 33)—that makes four times. The fifth time is Acts 1:5, where Jesus refers back to John's statement. The sixth is Acts 11:16, which refers again to what Jesus said about John's teaching. So these first six times all speak of John's announcement of Christ's baptizing with the Holy Spirit.

Now, the seventh time adds something new; it tells you who will receive this gift of Holy Spirit baptism. Notice carefully in verse 13 of 1 Corinthians 12 that this baptism is not a special gift for some extra godly Christians. This verse says, "For we were *all* baptized by one Spirit [circle that word *all*; underline it] into one body—whether Jews or Greeks, whether slaves or free." It doesn't have anything to do with our situation in life, whether we are superspiritual or not. *We were all made to drink of one Spirit.*

Two plus two equals four in everything but theology! Somehow, when you get to theology, it's a free-for-all! Some Christians say, "I don't know what theology says, but I believe so-and-so." Listen, theology is the study of God! Theology is the study of the Word of God! It's the queen of sciences. We want to be very careful to keep words clear and to use them only as God uses them.

First Corinthians 12:13 says that all Christians are baptized into the body of Christ by the Holy Spirit—that this is common to all Christians. The baptism of the Spirit is not anything to divide us into the "haves" and the "have-nots"—rather, all "have"! We are all united, according to God's Word, by our common baptism by the Holy Spirit into the Body of Christ.

Maybe some of the Corinthians were using the term *baptism of the Holy Spirit* as a "second work of grace" subsequent to conversion, and Paul is correcting this here. Look at the verbs in this verse: "For *we were* all baptized by one Spirit"—it's an aorist, or past tense—"we *were* baptized into the Body of Christ." When? When Jesus gloriously forgave your sins and placed you into His family. When you became His child, He identified you. He thrust you into the Body of Christ. If you want to use the meaning of the word as "immersed"—He immersed you forever into Christ. "For we were all baptized by one Spirit into one body." We *were* all made—past tense—as part of His Body to drink of that Spirit.

Baptism is a once-for-all happening, but the filling of the Holy Spirit—ah, my friend, the apostles were filled, and then they were filled, and then they were filled again—the same people—many times! There must be a continuous flowing of the Spirit of God upon your life. And it must be maintained with great care and openness to God and to His work in you. Let us be Spirit-filled Christians! Paul says, "Be 'being filled' with the Spirit" (see Eph. 5:18)—that's what it means. Keep on continually being filled with the Spirit.

The New Testament gives one huge cry for unity. Oh, it calls out for oneness! Jesus keeps telling us, "As the branches are one in the vine, as the sheep are one in the fold, as the building blocks are one in the building, be one in Me!" (See John 10:16 and 15:5.) It's a terrible thing to Jesus for the Body to be separated or divided.

We are all alike—but we are also all different. First Corinthians 12:4–5 says: "There are different gifts, but the same Spirit. There are different ministries, but the same Lord."

The human body is the illustration: it has many "members," or parts, and they're all different. Your ear is different from your hair; and your eye is different from your arm. This is what makes the body useful, and God says, "That's what I want you to be, together as My people. Just like that!"

There are four lists of the various gifts in the New Testament, and Paul gives them all—Romans 12; 1 Corinthians 12:8–10; 1 Corinthians 12:28–30; and another list in Ephesians 4. Twenty-nine different gifts are listed in all.

The gift of prophecy, or preaching, is in each of the various lists. (By the way, if you want to know what prophecy is, it's in 1 Corinthians 14:3: "The person who prophesies speaks to people for edification, encouragement, and consolation." It's just speaking out God's truth.) God also gives to the church teachers, evangelists, pastors, those who help others, and so on. I said to a man in my study the other day, "It's obvious to us all that God has given you the gift of helping others. We ask you to do something, and you do it 'yesterday!' And you seem to do it so easily and so joyously."

Remember, these gifts are supernatural. They are not just common talents. God may take a natural talent and endow it with the Holy Spirit at conversion so that the convert moves into a new orbit with that talent. Or He may "start from scratch," and as the new believer is baptized by the Spirit into the Body of Christ, he is given a new gift—or several.

I don't think the lists from these four sections of Scripture are meant to be all-inclusive. In our present space age, for example, God can add other gifts and expand the church. Maybe some are not as important as they used to be. But the same Spirit of God flows and works and moves and empowers the church; it makes the church glorify Christ and enables the members to help one another.

The thing I want you to see is this: No Christian should ever say, "I have no gift." That simply is not true. You can find your gift by seeing those things you do that are helpful to the rest of the believers, things you do with ease by the Spirit of God. Frankly, I don't know any place in the Scripture that tells us how to find what our gifts are. I suspect the Lord doesn't want us to get hung up on introspection and start taking aptitude tests. Evidently the

Spirit Who gives the gifts is the One who can easily tell you what yours are, and maybe tell your brother, too, in case you need his counsel about it.

But look at the list of the gifts and ask, "Lord, where do I serve in the Body?" And be glad for your gifts! Be glad for other people's gifts; rejoice in them. Fit yourself together with the Body of Christ.

Listen: to not use your gift is a terrible thing. To withhold yourself is like severing a portion of a body. If a hand is suddenly severed, it's shocking and repulsive! But when my hand is connected to my arm, and I reach it out to you and say, "Good morning, my friend," you think to yourself, *That's warm and good. I like that.*

Part of the last verse in 1 Corinthians 12 says, "Desire the greater gifts" (v. 31). I can't believe it means that all of us should get whatever we want. This passage already said the gifts are given to us as the Spirit wills. But rather, as a Body of believers—it's a plural thought—we should desire the gifts among our particular group that are the best gifts for us, those that are going to help us minister to our area and around the world in great power. God isn't making "big shots," my friend; He's interested in making people fit into the family of God and make the work of the gospel "go."

And He says the way is love. "I will show you an even better way" (v. 31b).

Listen: whatever you know as a Christian, you don't know much yet if you haven't learned the exhilaration of "putting it together" in the Spirit with other believers, of humbling yourself to say, "I'm one with you, my brother." Be bold enough and full of faith enough to say, "Look, here's what I am. Here's what I can contribute. I'll submit to whatever way the rest of you in the Body want to use me!"

chapter eight
BE A CHRISTIAN WIFE

*W*e live in an age of innovation. Years ago the book *Future Shock* accurately predicted the fracture of the family that was to come: "The flood of novelty about to crash down upon us will spread from university and research center into the home. Penetrating deep into our private lives, it will place absolutely unprecedented strains on the family itself."[1]

And it certainly has.

We need to go to the Scriptures and see what God has to say to us about the home and the family, to steady us for these days. The family is the smallest unit of the church, and if we're going to be committed to the Body, our first challenge is to those right under our own roof.

First Peter 3:1–6 is especially for the women: "Wives, in the same way, submit yourselves to your own husbands so that even if some disobey the Christian message, they may be won over without a message by the way their wives live, when they observe your pure, reverent lives. Your beauty should not be the outward beauty of elaborate hairstyles and the wearing of gold ornaments or of fine clothes; rather, it should be an inner beauty with the imperishability of a gentle and quiet spirit, which is very valuable in God's eyes. For in the past, the holy women who hoped in God also beautified themselves in this way, submitting to their own husbands, just as Sarah obeyed Abraham, calling him lord. You have become her children when you do good and aren't frightened by anything alarming."

A feminist group recently built a big bonfire and tossed into it different so-called "enslaving" items. One was a Bible! Probably they had never read it, or if they had, they hadn't understood it. For the Bible puts us *all* under authority, under orders. It isn't as though the woman is supposed to be mealy-mouthed, crouching, and unrespected, with the man towering over her. No, no! The Bible puts us all under orders. Moms and dads, husbands and wives, children, young people—all of us have our places in the plan of God for the home.

Be aware of the weight of those first words of 1 Peter 3: "Wives, in the same way, . . ." And in verse 7, "Husbands, in the same way, . . ."

This is going to open up the whole thing to us, so let's concentrate on those words, "In the same way."

There are three situations in 1 Peter that set the stage for the husband-wife relationship of chapter 3. First, 2:11–14 concerns citizens under any government: "Dear friends, I urge you . . . conduct yourselves honorably among the Gentiles . . . that . . . they may, by observing your good works, glorify God in a day of visitation. Submit to every human institution because of the Lord, whether to the Emperor as the supreme authority, or to governors as those sent out by him to punish those who do evil and to praise those who do good."

Citizens, says God, live as gentle people, as those who are submissive. This is strong language when you consider the cruelty of the Roman government at the time these words were written!

Second, 2:18 concerns slaves under any kind of master: "Household slaves, submit yourselves to your masters with all respect."

Think what would happen to a business if everyone did just what he pleased. You can see the common sense of this in any organized structure. But, my friend, think when these words were written! These were slaves, often in chains. Now read on, verses 18–20: "Submit yourselves to your masters . . . not only to the good and gentle but also to the cruel. For it brings favor if, because of conscience toward God, someone endures grief from suffering unjustly. For what credit is there if you endure when you sin and are beaten? But when you do good and suffer, if you endure, it brings favor with God."

So far Peter has given us two bundles of dynamite—but now this third illustration is his atomic bomb. Verses 21–23: "For you were called to this, because Christ also suffered for you, leaving you an example, so that you should follow in His steps. He did not commit sin, and no deceit was found in His mouth; when reviled, He did not revile in return; when suffering, He did not threaten, but committed Himself to the One who judges justly."

Amazing! When God tells either a wife or a husband to be submissive in marriage, His "in the same way" refers back to citizens under cruel Rome, slaves with ruthless masters, and Jesus on the cross!

All other human relationships should also take Christ as the example of how we are to respond and submit. How could God tell us more strongly? Jesus' earthly life was hard and difficult. Life is hard, isn't it? Many times people aren't fair in dealing with others. Many times they aren't even humane!

So in the midst of this, how should you react? Like Jesus. He entrusted Himself to Him who judges justly. He gave Himself to God.

Interesting that when we look at Ephesians 5, another section speaking to husbands and wives, it also is surrounded by illustrations of other situations where we have to submit, and the conclusion to the whole thing seems to be Ephesians 5:21: "Submitting to one another in the fear of Christ."

That means everybody is to submit! Phillips' translation puts it: "'Fit in with' each other, because of your common reverence for Christ."

We are called to humility. We are called to bend our necks in obedience to Christ, to be reasonable and generous, and to give of ourselves. This is God's way for us all, whatever our position in the home or in society.

First Peter 3 says: "Wives, in the same way, . . ." God is going to show us how to be His beautiful people. Verses 1–6 in particular tell how to be God's beautiful woman.

The instruction in verse 1 is to be submissive to your husband. Dear lady, don't be afraid of this. You say, "To him? You've got to be kidding!" Yes, that's right, to *him!* Nobody else. Take your place as a woman of God. (Although, in a sense, both parties have to be submissive: the husband has to submit to his role as leader because God has asked it of him, and God will help him.)

"Adapt yourselves to your husbands" is the way Phillips puts it. Literally, stand under him. Support him, uphold him, lift him. Be his woman! And it says, "Do it willingly." It doesn't say, "Wives, when your husband says so, be submissive to him." No, it says this is what you are to offer him, to give to him—not reluctantly, but joyously.

It's the first step toward beauty! And it's a wonderful step. It's like a dive into a pool on a hot summer day. There's a shock at first, but after that it feels so good! That's the way God's will is: it may shock you at first. Indeed, to talk like this is shocking in a day when there is so much rebellion. "But afterward it yields the peaceable fruits of righteousness" (see Heb. 12:11).

There are two reasons why this makes you a beautiful woman. The first is what it does to your man. God has built into every man the need to be a responsible leader. If you take that away from him, you deny him his manhood. You ruin him; you squelch him.

Something important happens to a man on the day of his wedding. I've talked to many a man just beforehand, and he says something like, "Wow! I'm taking on quite a responsibility, aren't I?" It hits him! Sometimes we pretty much have to prop him up and hold him together until the wedding starts! But he's thinking hard. To himself he says, "I'm taking a woman into my life—my woman. I'll have to care for her, watch out for her, protect her, clothe her, make sure that she has what she needs. This is my woman!" It's a wonderful thing for a man to say, "Now I have a wife!"

But God says that for him to perform this inbuilt, dignified duty well, you wives must offer yourselves to him. You must relax and let him lead.

Some men are reluctant. I don't know what happened in their background—they're just reluctant to be leaders in their home. They often will defer to you. Women, you will have to say, "No, my dear, you lead. It is God's way. You'll make a good leader! Come on, take hold of the leadership of our home." You must talk about it, pray about it, and then act on it. Submit yourself to him. Give him that leadership.

This is so revolutionary! It is so wonderful! It will never be done unless you are a Christian. But if you've received Jesus Christ, you will get from Him that inner strength. "Wives, in the same way, submit yourselves to your own husbands so that even if some disobey the Christian message," they will be saved.

Some of the wives to whom Peter wrote became Christians after they were married. (The Bible always says that no Christian should marry a non-Christian. That's being "unequally yoked." Don't say, "But I've prayed about it." You're praying about something the Bible says flatly is not in the works for the Christian.)

Yet to those wives who were converted after they were married, Peter says, "Now, look: if your husband doesn't obey the Word of God, he may be won without a word by the behavior of his wife."

If you have a non-Christian husband, don't whine, "All right now, Charlie, we're gonna go to church. Put on your shirt. And we're gonna read the Bible every day." No, no! You can't nag him into the kingdom of God!

The will of God is that you win him *without a word* because of your sweet, submissive life.

What your submission does to your man is so important.

The second reason submission makes you beautiful is a strictly personal, internal reason: what it does to you as a woman. It's true that "there is no Jew or Greek, slave or free, male or female; for you are all one in Christ Jesus" (Gal. 3:28). In Christ Jesus, God sees us in the family. But as family members we have our various roles, and it is important that you fit into your function, your role, in the home.

Women are equal, my friend. It fact, women are more "equal" than men—no doubt about it! We men know that. But you don't have to be *alike* to be equal. God has taken people equal in His heart, equal in His family, equal in society, and put them into different roles. The husband is to submit to God as the leader of the home. The woman is to submit to God in following her husband.

The early church father Chrysostom said, "A masterly wife is as much to be despised and derided for taking rule over her husband as he is for yielding to it."

Notice how it is that a submissive wife becomes beautiful inwardly. Many Bible translations speak of her "pure, reverent" behavior. The King James Version says her behavior is "chaste." That's a good word.

"Your beauty should not be the outer beauty of elaborate hairstyles and the wearing of gold ornaments or of fine clothes; rather, it should be an inner beauty with the imperishability of a gentle and quiet spirit, which is very valuable in God's eyes" (1 Pet. 3:3–4).

God made you with a feel for beauty, ladies. He did not make us men with much of that. Good taste in the home, good taste as a person, is a special gift from God—this feel for outward beauty. But how about inward beauty?

What does Peter mean by "chaste" behavior? Well, you women will know that in fashion, for instance, a chaste dress is without frills; it's simple but elegant. It's understated; it's quiet; its quality is understood. Now, that's the way a woman's life is to be. A chaste life is simple and modest; not confused, but directed by God. She knows where she's going and what God wants her to be.

Men, I believe that we have a responsibility to make our ladies elegant. Marriages need good manners. We men are the ones who should offer our ladies tact and consideration. Where we love people the most, we should be the most polite. So many times we come home and throw our feelings around and hurt and wound. Let us acknowledge right now before God and one another that that is sin! It's a terrible failure to be nicer to the secretaries at our jobs than to our wives.

And this little wife, if she isn't becoming beautiful on the inside, will start to panic and put it on the outside instead.

I sometimes go to *Word Studies in the New Testament,* an old book by Marvin R. Vincent. He says that in the time of the Roman Empire, fashions were going to an alarming extreme. How about this?

The Roman women of the day were addicted to ridiculous extravagance in the adornment of the hair.

Juvenal, in his satire, talks about these customs. He says, "The attendants will vote on the dressing of the hair as if a question of reputation or of life were at stake, so great is the trouble she takes in quest of beauty; with so many tiers does she load, with so many continuous stories does she build up high on her head. She is as tall as an Amazon in front, behind she is shorter. You would think her another person from behind.

"The hair was dyed, and secured with costly pins and with nets of gold thread."

And then I read this last sentence, and nearly fell off my chair: "False hair and blonde wigs were worn"![2] With our billion-dollar cosmetic business, women today aren't much different.

Now, I'll be the first to agree that outward beauty is really important. It's lovely; it's appreciated. Ladies, for the sake of your husband, your friends, and your Lord, you should look as attractive as possible. One cosmetic ad reads, "Women who let themselves go, wake up to find their husbands gone." Another says, "There are no ugly women, only lazy ones."

But the Bible says to give the greatest attention to your heart—that "hidden person," where there should be the imperishable jewels of "a gentle and quiet spirit, which is very valuable in God's eyes." God wants to look into your heart and see jewels glittering! God's woman is to be jeweled within!

And God's woman is to make her home out of that spirit that is quiet and gentle and meek. Houses are made of sticks and stones, but homes are made of gentle things like the hearts of women turned to Jesus.

My friend, meekness is not weakness. It is strength under control. You read from the last chapter of Proverbs about the godly woman, and you say, "My, she has to be a strong woman!" You women who care for our children and our homes—sometimes with outside work as well—you have to be strong and wise, and willing to take on a great deal of work. Proverbs 31 says,

A good wife, who can find?
    She is far more precious than jewels.
The heart of her husband trusts in her,
    and he will have no lack of gain.
She does him good, and not harm,
    all the days of her life.
She seeks wool and flax,
    and works with willing hands.
She is like the ships of the merchant,
    she brings her food from afar.

She rises while it is yet night
and provides food for her household
and tasks for her maidens. (vv. 10–15 RSV)

And then it all ends with these lovely verses:
Charm is deceitful, and beauty is vain,
but a woman who fears the LORD is to be praised.
Give her of the fruit of her hands,
and let her works praise her in the gates. (vv. 30–31)

Women must be managers in purchasing, and wise in their duties in the home. God bless you women!

The closing illustration of the portion in 1 Peter is Sarah: "For in the past, the holy women who hoped in God also beautified themselves in this way, submitting to their own husbands, just as Sarah obeyed Abraham, calling him lord. You have become her children when you do good and aren't frightened by anything alarming" (1 Pet. 3:5–6).

"Calling him lord"! Sarah called her husband "lord." This is a crazy story, but I've got to tell you about the woman who crawled into bed one night. She yawned and said, "Lord, I'm tired!" And her husband said, "My dear, in the privacy of our home you can call me Jack."

I don't think this man caught the spirit of 1 Peter 3! The word _lord_ originally meant "sir" or "master." According to the Book of Genesis, Sarah referred to Abraham this way in a prayer to God, when Abraham wasn't even around. In other words, it wasn't a phony thing; it was the way she truly thought about him.

Sarah herself, by the way, was outwardly, in her physical appearance, a knockout. At sixty-five she was taken by an Egyptian pharaoh to be part of his harem. At ninety, the king of the Philistines tried to take her! Even so, they didn't know her real beauty. Thousands of years later, God records for us in 1 Peter that her *true* beauty was her attitude—a quiet and meek and peaceable spirit. Her secret is found in verse 5: She "hoped in God." This is the way women get more beautiful as they get older. Their great spirit is seen upon them.

Whether their husbands deserve it or not, women are to trust in God and be God's woman. I'd like to challenge you: Do you want to go God's way, or do you want to go on clawing for your own way? Christian woman, trust Him to make you exactly what He wants you to be. Ask Him to bring you to a new, submissive attitude, taking on your role with dignity and charm and beauty— before God and your husband and your family.

The Lord will honor you for this! And He will also make you truly beautiful.

chapter nine
BE A CHRISTIAN HUSBAND

I read somewhere that the famous historian Edward Gibbon once wrote, "Nations may survive military defeat, depression, famine, flood, fire, and governmental changes; but when homes break down, so do schools, churches, government, and everything else that is worthwhile."

The home is in crisis in our world today. Every marriage has its difficult times. If it weren't so crucial to our lives, we wouldn't care! But in your home when you win, you really win; and when you lose, you really lose. And the scars are never superficial.

So it's important that we come to the Word of God about the home. First Peter 3:1–6 talks about the wife. And then verse 7: "Husbands, in the same way, live with your wives with understanding of their weaker nature yet showing them honor as coheirs of the grace of life, that your prayers will not be hindered."

Preaching and writing are a dangerous business, especially on the subject of marriage. You come under the judgment of the message yourself!

I was studying 1 Peter this week, and as I was working away, my wife said, "What are you doing?"

I said, "I'm putting together this chapter on the husband to turn in next Tuesday to the editor."

She said, "Then you've got six days to shape up!"

The word *husband* comes to us from the verb "to husband," "to keep carefully." A husband should be one who tends his family with great care. A husbandman—as the Bible often uses that term—is a farmer who tends his crops. Jesus said, "I am the true Vine, and My Father is the Husbandman" (see John 15:1). Now, as God the Father nurtures and cares for His beloved Vine, so the husband is to care for his dear family.

To the Jew, the husband was the foundation of the whole household. Still today, Abraham is "our father Abraham." And Abraham had the twelve great-grandsons who became the fathers of the twelve tribes. These families grew very fast, into hundreds and thousands. Within each tribe, each husband was to be God's man to his own family. He sacrificed for their sins as well as for his own. He was responsible for their care, and also for their behavior. When all Israel convened, the husband would stand out in front of his family, with all his family members behind him. If the family had been a disgrace, he was a disgrace. For instance, the reason God said of Reuben "you are unstable as water" is because his family had not done well. They were humiliated, and Reuben was humiliated. The father answered *for them;* they answered *to him.*

To say, "I am a husband" in the light of God's history is to say a great deal.

The introductory phrase of this seventh verse of 1 Peter 3 says, "Husbands, . . . live with your wives with understanding." "Live with them"; in other words, don't allow unnecessary separations. You married partners are to be so unified in your spirits that you don't even put "his" and "hers" on your towels!

Phillips' translation has a good rendering for the words *with*

understanding. He says, "Try to understand the wives you live with."
(I'm glad he put "try" in there! It is hard at times, isn't it, men?)

I ask young bridegrooms that I counsel, "Now, do you feel
that you really understand her?" The fellow usually scratches his
head and says, "Well, Pastor, not really." And I say, "You're average!
It's all right." All people are rather complex. None of us ever
understands everything, even about ourselves, let alone about
other people.

I love what James Henry Jowett has to say about this phrase
"with understanding," or as the King James Version says, "according to knowledge":

Let us call it the atmosphere of reasonableness.
"According to knowledge." We may grasp its content
by proclaiming its opposite: "Dwell with your wives
according to ignorance. Just walk in blindness. Don't
look beyond your own desires. Let your vision be
entirely introspective and microscopic. Never exercise
your eyes in clear and comprehensive outlook. Dwell
in ignorance!"

"No," says the apostle, "dwell according to knowledge." Keep your eyes open. Let reason be alert and
active. Let all your behavior be governed by a sweet
reasonableness. Don't let appetite determine a doing.
Don't let thy personal wish have the first and last
word. Exalt thy reason! Give sovereignty to thy reason! Be thoughtful and unceasingly considerate.

It is the absence of this prevailing spirit of reasonableness which has marred and murdered many a
bright and fair-promising communion. He is not
really bad at heart, but he doesn't think! He dwells
according to ignorance; his reason is asleep, and the
beautiful, delicate tie of wedded fellowship is smitten,
wounded, and eventually destroyed.[1]

What rich words!

So Peter says, "Husbands, in the same way, live with your wives with understanding." He then gives three reasons why you should. First, live with your wife with understanding because she is "the weaker partner" (1 Pet. 3:7 NIV); second, because you are "co-heirs of the grace of life"; and third, because if you don't, your prayers will be hindered.

First of all, your wife is physically weaker. I say "physically" because I'm sure that that's the meaning of it. Phillips translates it this way, and I think he's right. It doesn't say that women are weaker; we know very well that in many areas they are much stronger. But their bodies are usually weaker. The King James Version uses the word "vessel," which comes from the word we use for "vase." (If it's very expensive, it's "vahse." Most of you women are "vahses.") It's a lovely receptacle that covers and contains important things. You mark a vase: "Fragile—Handle with Care." From _vessel_ we also get our word "vest" or "vestment"—a piece of outer garment. So the woman's physical body, her encasement, is generally weaker than a man's.

This is why Peter says that it is reasonable for the Christian man to watch over his more delicate wife.

In some non-Christian cultures the men go down to the market square, sit around and talk, and smoke water pipes while the women are out following the oxen or the buffalo with a plow. We say, "How awful!"

Well, in the Western world a large percentage of our married women work. They work all day long; then they come home and do cooking and cleaning and washing and so on. A recent magazine did a survey on this, and they found that husbands whose wives work do almost as little around the house as husbands whose wives don't work. I think one practical application of this phrase in 1 Peter is that we men should pitch in at home, especially if the wife works. When a wife must work, then the husband and children must also work in that home. Dwell reasonably with your wife. Often she has a weaker back, weaker feet, and so on.

I've seen some husbands who actually get irritated when their wives get sick, and all the kids are home, and they have to do the housework. "What is she doing getting sick on me like that? Leaving me all this mess!" The kids are climbing all over the place and the guy is saying, "Let me go back to work!" They're almost insulted that their wife would dare get sick on them.

"Live with her with understanding"—that's what God's man will do.

I remember when Anne and I had our first baby, Sherry, in Tacoma, Washington. My mother-in-law came from Pennsylvania to help take care of Anne when she came home from the hospital. I met her at the plane and I said, "Oh, it was great! It was really a pretty easy birth!" Mother said, "Humph, *you've* never had a baby!"

"To husband" means to watch her as you would a flowering plant. I said the word originally meant "gardener." To husband your wife means to protect her, tend her, feed her, watch over her.

This is Christian love in action. This is wise love. I like what Matthew Henry has to say in volume 6 of his *Commentary* about honoring the wife: "Giving due respect to her, and maintaining her authority, protecting her person, supporting her credit, delighting in her conversation, affording her a handsome maintenance, and placing a due trust and confidence in her."

Beautiful!

Everybody dreams about the perfect man and the perfect woman. I asked one of our young girls, "What kind of a person do you want to marry?" She giggled for awhile, and she never really came out with it. It's hard, you know, because there isn't any perfect person. That well-known Christian writer Keith Miller says that his ideal wife would be a combination of Mother Theresa, Elizabeth Taylor, and Betty Crocker!

Let's remember that in our households we live with people who are imperfect. They're still sinners—we've got to allow for that fact. The standards God gives, we often fail to meet. They should not be taken lightly, but we often fail with them.

The second reason Peter says husbands should "live according to knowledge" with their wives is because you are equally heirs of the grace of life. What a beautiful phrase! Look at it again: "Heirs of the grace of life." The phrase is even written into the marriage ceremony that many ministers use: "By His apostles He has instructed those who enter in this relation to cherish a mutual esteem and love; to bear with each other's infirmities and weaknesses; to comfort each other in sickness, trouble, and sorrow; in honesty and industry to provide for each other and for their household in temporal things; and to live together as the heirs of the grace of life."

I love to think of that. When these two are truly Christian, both have received God's grace in Christian marriage. Through the years, they receive together those heart-filling benefits of God, those streams of living water. It's all of God. They never deserve it. They never earn it.

I said to a couple recently, "Your children are such a blessing. What wonderful young people!" And the response was the response of 90 percent of us: "Oh, it's just God's grace! We didn't do everything right; we made a lot of mistakes. God is gracious."

"Heirs together of the grace of life"—that's the thrill of living together with God. Grace upon grace, the exceeding abundance of His grace! Grace that comes and comes and comes again—that's what we get when we live together as the heirs of the grace of God. Then, you see, His grace is the strength that unifies, pulls together, pushes on, and makes your home really "work."

The word *heir* in 1 Peter 3:7 indicates that we're recipients together of an inheritance from one who has died. But it's not the idea of a lump-sum payment; it's wealth that keeps coming and coming from the riches of that person who died.

Jesus Christ has died for us. His grace, His wealth, keeps coming and coming in continuous payments. We are heirs together, in Christian marriage, of that grace of life. Listen: if you've never come to the place of receiving Jesus Christ in your home, you don't know the riches of His grace that abound to those who are under His marvelous goodness. My friend, you need Jesus! You need His amazing, cementing power in your marriage. You need to become "heirs together of the grace of life."

According to Israel's Old Testament law, every couple in the first year of marriage had a special benefit: the husband was never allowed to go to war. I suppose they thought he was so in love, he would make a poor fighter anyway. But it was a thoughtfulness on the part of the fathers of Israel, and on God Himself as He gave the law, that there was allowed an adjustment period when they'd learn to become not "I," but "we."

The first years of marriage—they're wonderful. Ten years go by; love grows. Twenty years go by, thirty, fifty—couples look back and say, "Dear, you didn't know anything about me then compared to now. My, how did you ever have the nerve to marry me?" And she replies (I hope she does!), "Wisest thing I ever did!"

But some marriages grow cold. I have a cartoon in front of me. It shows the husband sitting behind his paper and his wife sitting across the room with her hands folded, looking wistful. Obviously, she's just been questioning him. He puts his paper down and says, "Of course I love you. I'm your husband. That's my duty."

Married love should be like life on an ocean liner that goes plowing through the water. You wake up in the morning together, you go through the day's activities, you go to bed together at night, you wake up the next morning—but you're not in the same spot you were yesterday morning. Your ship has been steaming through the water toward its destination. Marriage should be like that, with the growth and the progress of love.

Of course every marriage goes along in gains and losses, gains and losses. But there should be great overall gain—that growing sense of heirdom of the grace of life.

Years ago a wonderful Christian couple wrote us in their old age, and they felt sorry for us because we weren't there yet! We couldn't see all the good things they saw. They said, "Someday you'll enter into the rich years!" As Browning wrote,

Grow old along with me:
The best is yet to be—
The last for which the first was made.

Marriage is too rewarding ever to be completely finished. It must be a growing, developing relationship.

The third reason you husbands should live with your wives according to careful understanding is because if you don't, your prayers will be hindered.

The Greek word for *hinder* was used, for instance, in warfare, when one army might seek to hinder the approach of the other army by cutting a ditch in the road upon which they were advancing. Peter is saying that the husband is to live wisely and reasonably because if he does not, his very life will be a roadblock to spiritual progress, a barrier on the road of the way to God. You won't even be able to pray right if you don't live right at home!

Men, I wonder how much prayer in this world has been thwarted because of the way you live at home! This word *hinder* indicates that the unreasonable man will find prayer tedious. It doesn't mean he will never pray; it indicates that he will be detained from praying. Could this be the reason that your prayer life, Dad, is not what it ought to be? Because you're wrong at home? "It's a strange thing," you say, "I just don't feel like praying." Of course you don't feel like praying! Or, what you pray has no power, and you just "say your prayers," without heart.

One of the great needs of the Body of Christ is for the men to go to God fervently in concentrated prayer. I'm amazed at how really little praying we do—when we say it's so important! "Ask, and it shall be given you; seek, and ye shall find; knock, and it shall be opened unto you" (Matt. 7:7 KJV; see also v. 8). With all the Scriptures about prayer, I'm amazed at the little prayer. I wonder if the reason isn't that the men in our families are living below the standard of the Word of God. Why are they not better pray-ers? Because they need to be better husbands. I speak to myself. "We have not, because we ask not. We ask not, because we ask amiss" (see James 4:2–3). And the reason we ask amiss, says James, is that our lives are wrong.

Husbands, fathers, when you don't give yourselves to fervent, disciplined prayer, your family suffers, and the world suffers. There will be a lack of communication and spirit in your home. No wonder our kids are often unmanageable! When there's a lack of discipline and heart and joy in the home, there will be the same lack everywhere else. You ask the average school teacher if kids today, generally speaking, show personal discipline and ambition and high morale—the results of a good home life and the strong backing of prayer. Why, some of these teachers practically have to fend for their lives.

To have little or no contact with God, Dad, reaps devastating fruit. To bypass God is to ask for trouble for yourself, your loved wife, your children, your church, and your nation. I wonder how much trouble we are experiencing in our land today because men cannot pray.

You may say, "Well, I'm just not a man of prayer." You can't be a man of prayer until you are God's kind of man for your wife. "Live with your wives with understanding." Live with her as a man of God. As Ephesians says, "Husbands, love your wives, just as also Christ loved the church and gave Himself for her" (5:25). Then you can pray!

What should you do? Repent! Change your mind. Change your direction. Go home and say, "Look, I have not been what I ought to be, and I want to be God's man for this home." You're His gift to that home! Live there with understanding of the Book of God. Provide spiritual food and stability. You can't be wrong at home and be right with God.

You can be a godly husband; you can become a praying husband. There's not a man who can't be this by the grace of God, not one. God's grace is sufficient. It's available to you again, and again, and again, and again.

"If any man lack wisdom"—if any man needs to know how to live with his wife with understanding—*The Living Bible* says, "Ask Him! And He will gladly tell you, for He is always ready to give a bountiful supply of wisdom to all who ask Him. He will not resent it" (James 1:5).

chapter ten

PUT TOGETHER
A CHRISTIAN
HOME

*T*here were two porcupines living in Alaska. It was very cold. To keep warm, they decided to draw close together. But when they did that, they needled each other. So they pulled apart. But again they got cold. And so they moved close again, and they got needled. Poor porcupines! They were continuously either cold or needling one another.

That's the way some people live in their homes. At a distance they are lonely and cold. But when they draw near, they needle and hurt each other.

I don't believe we need to live that way. I believe God wants us to be able to draw close and be very warm and comfortable together.

But there are obstacles to this unity that I'm talking about. Just let me reconstruct for you what happens in the average home.

When you get married, there is just one person that you really have to satisfy. And even that isn't always easy!

Perhaps the husband comes from a big family. He's noisy, eats huge meals, ransacks the refrigerator all the time. And he's a very easygoing fellow. Where he grew up, everyone came and went when they wished and ate when they wanted.

But she, you see, was an only child. Hers was a very quiet, orderly home. Everybody was restrained.

Then they were married. They have trouble! Soon he's singing that old song,

Why don't we get along?
Everything I do is wrong;
Tell me, what's the reason
I'm not pleasin' you?

Well, as we've heard, "It takes a heap o' living to make a house a home." And it takes plain work to build unity into any marriage.

G. K. Chesterton, that wise Roman Catholic philosopher, said, "I have known many marriages, but never a compatible one." What he meant was this, that when people come together, there's already a built-in, ready-made incompatibility. They come from different backgrounds and different ways of doing things. It takes a lifetime of work to keep adjusting to one another.

One counselor said, "Every variety of marriage, if it is to be successful and enduring, has one requirement. . . . Two people shall be ready to sink themselves in the creation of a new unit bigger than either of them. The creation must be important to them. They must accept their relationship as the permanent framework of their lives."

A married couple has only one personal interpersonal relationship—until the first child comes. But then there are *three* interpersonal relationships that can go awry: mother and dad, baby and mother, and baby and dad.

But think of it when two children come into that home. That means there are six interpersonal relationships that have to be kept clear. That's nothing! Think of it when four children are in that home: then there are fifteen interpersonal relationships that can get out of focus. And if there are five children, there are twenty-one interpersonal relationships that can go awry! With six, there are twenty-eight! Now, how many must you adjust to in *your* home? How many people must adjust to you? Think about it. Each relationship is important—and potentially devastating!

You know, when a beloved member of the family leaves, one of the comments is, "It's sure quiet around here, isn't it?" You know why? Because a lot of interpersonal relationships have just walked out the door.

Recently I left home for three weeks, and I took away four interpersonal relationships from our home. When my plane flew away, so did trouble! Interpersonal relationships in the Ortlund household went down from ten to six. Things got a lot simpler!

Now, think what happens when grandparents come to visit a family of, let's say, six. Suddenly they have twenty-eight interpersonal relationships! The kids say, "Hey, what's going on around here?"

But think of it another way. A family of six comes into the quiet little home of Grandmother and Grandfather. Things have been so quiet, so serene—and suddenly, instead of one, they have twenty-eight interpersonal relationships to contend with in that home! They love their family, but when they all go, the grandparents look at each other and sigh, "Phew-w-w-w!" And Granddad says to Grandmother, "I guess I'm getting old." No, Granddad, you just had twenty-seven interpersonal relationships walk in on you. That's a whirlwind!

And suppose instead of the "classic" family, you have one that's blended? *She* got used to being a single parent, and then suddenly she not only has a new husband but his kids too. Or *he* got used to raising just his own, and suddenly there are all these new bodies under his roof! And no wonder the children are bewildered and upset.

And yet home is a place where we have to work on all those interpersonal relationships. Home is where there ought to be peace because you count it as the most important place in all the world.

In an old _Life_ magazine I read:

The business man gives service with a smile: he is deferential to his boss, his customers, and usually even to his underlings. Women are polite to their neighbors and to door-to-door salesmen. Hardly a voice is raised in anger except behind the closed door of the home. As the outside world becomes more and more constrained, more and more people seem to feel that the home is the last remaining place where they can quit kidding and be their own ornery selves. The bride and groom who have been standing so patiently in the reception line, smiling sweetly at people they hardly know (and some people they know and don't like) can seem ornery indeed to each other when they get home and let down their hair.

Isn't that true? Haven't you caught yourself being mean at home but sweet to everybody else? There are plenty of obstacles—but we need to change the spirit in our homes to loving unity.

So, how do you do this? There are three progressive steps:

Number One: Realize you already have something going for you in the very makeup of the home. God created the family. God is the One who thought of it all. First He made a man. Then He criticized His own creation by saying, "It is not good for man to live alone." The first thing about creation that God said was "not good" was man's aloneness. So He gave man a woman! He began human life with a family.

Then, remember, life got pretty mean on this earth. God sent the flood, and then He gave this world a new start with Noah and his family. God began again with a family.

Then God chose a nation, Israel—as we read in Genesis 12. And when He did, He began with a family. God loves families. He just loves the home! Read the Scriptures and you see it there. In God's economy, the family is the basic unity.

There's a oneness in the family already there by address alone—you live in the same place. There's oneness by your name, by the kind of food you eat. You have oneness because of the memories that are built together. From the very beginning, little Junior begins to walk like his daddy, and the children begin to talk like their parents. After awhile, Mother and Dad even begin to look alike.

Number Two: We get unity in our home life by a definite step of faith. We must believe in the Lord Jesus Christ. When we've done that, God begins right there and gives us a deeper unity. He places us into the Body of Christ so that the members of the family, having trusted in the Lord Jesus, have a new relationship in depth. They are in the family of God—brothers and sisters in Christ. They have the same Holy Spirit. They have the same Lord. The Christian home has a lot going for it! It is a wonderful, new thing God does when we believe. The Christian home is the Christian church in miniature!

Let's look together at some Scriptures. First, Ephesians 4:1–3 tells us, "I, therefore, the prisoner in the Lord, urge you to walk worthy of the calling you have received." Now, how do you lead a life that builds unity into the church and, in our case, the church in the home? He says you are to lead a life "with all humility and gentleness, with patience, accepting one another in love, diligently keeping the unity of the Spirit with the peace that binds us." Notice that word *keep* or *maintain*. Be eager to keep it! We should cherish and nourish this unity. We should love it and live as if we are really in this unity. Mother and Father, your children are also your brothers and sisters in Christ. Young people, your Christian parents are your brothers and sisters in Christ.

The Christian home has intensified relationships. It's a little church. This is the idea we have in Ephesians 5, beginning with verse 28: "In the same way, husbands should love their wives as their own bodies. He who loves his wife loves himself. For no one ever hates his flesh, but provides and cares for it, just as Christ does the church, since we are members of His body. 'For this reason a man will leave his father and mother and be joined to his wife, and the two will become one flesh.'"

I received help on this in my study this week. In a book by W. J. Fields, I read:

This concept has profound implications.

Husbands and wives often think of their spouses as their "other partner" in marriage. They think of themselves as two individuals who have contracted to live together as man and wife, each a completely separate entity with his own rights, privileges and desires.

Paul's concept goes far beyond that. He feels very strongly that the marriage state is a unity. From his way of looking at things there are not two individuals constituting a marriage; rather, each individual is a part of the other. Instead of being two separate individuals, they are two parts of one unity, each of which is necessary to make the unity complete.

In marriage there is a "one flesh" relationship, and married people are "therefore no more twain, but one flesh" (Matt. 19:6). One's wife is really not the "other" in marriage; she is her husband's "other self," his *alter ego*—inseparably bound and tied to him in love. One's husband is really not the "other" in marriage; he is his wife's "other self," her *alter ego*—inseparably bound and tied to her in love.

Therefore when the husband loves his wife, he is
not loving another person at all. He is loving a part of
himself. When the wife loves her husband, she is not
loving another person. She is loving a part of herself.[1]

Number Three: Build unity in your home by *obedience.* A man
takes his place as head of the house; the woman takes her place as
the mother and wife of the home. And the children remain children—obedient and loving. In other words, we take our God-
assigned roles in the family relationship.

"The husband," says Ephesians 5:23, "is head of the wife as also
Christ is head of the church. He is the Savior of the body."

Verse 25: "Husbands, love your wives, just as also Christ loved
the church and gave Himself for her."

Christ died for us! In a sense, the husband is to die to his own
desires and his own dreams. He is to reject his own comforts and
his own interests because the ones he loves the most deserve his
attention. He is willing to give himself to his family and for his
family. That's what Christ did!

Then he is to lead the family. If he loves right, he will lead
right. No man is to be the tyrant in his house, but every man is to
be head of his house.

One of our big problems today is that fathers are afraid to be
the head. The average man knows his wife is smarter than he is. But
we are still the head of the house! God has called us to leadership,
and we are to take it. Step into it!

I don't imagine that there are many parents who don't realize
their children are also pretty bright. And as they get older, they
know a lot more about some things than the parents know. But
you are still parents! There comes a time, Dad, when you must say
to your sixteen-year-old son, as you stand nose-to-nose, "I'm the
head of the house. I want you to know this, son. I don't spank you
anymore, but I'm the head." In the long run he's going to love your
leadership. You say to him, "I love you too much to let you go

astray." And you get on your knees with that son, and you watch God work unity into your home. The average boy is looking for that kind of leadership.

Dad, you are the God-appointed head of the house. Don't forget that position. Love and lead.

Ephesians 5:22 says: "Wives, submit to your own husbands as to the Lord."

An interviewer was talking to a couple on a television show recently. He asked the woman, "And who is the head of your house?" She said, "My husband is." The interviewer thought he'd be clever, so he said, "And who decided that?" She replied, "I did."

Ho, ho, ho! That was to be the cue for a big guffaw. But actually, you see, she's absolutely right. No one else could decide it. The husband is not to demand leadership; the wife is to *give* it. She is to submit to her place, and he is to take his place.

Mothers and dads, husbands and wives, talk about your roles! Talk about how you want to improve your romance, how you want to run your house, how you want to bring up your children—all these things. You've got to talk it out and find biblical ways to build unity into your home.

Ephesians 6:1–2 says, "Children, obey your parents in the Lord, because this is right. 'Honor your father and mother'—which is the first commandment with a promise."

Of course, as the children get older, wise parents begin to loosen the reins a bit and let the children assume more responsibilities. But essentially, the wise parent expects his child to obey, and the wise young person expects to obey—until he leaves father and mother and cleaves to his wife. Then he is to set up his own family with those same standards he learned while a child in his own home.

Children are to *honor* their parents. There's no age limit on that: as long as God lets you have your mother and father, honor them! After they're gone, honor their memory. Every home should display a picture of grandmother and grandfather. Let those children growing up look into the eyes of those grandparents, to remember their faith and to remember their heritage.

The young people who are growing up among us today have a different challenge than we've ever had. The world has been thrown at them all at once. I read the following in the magazine _Christian Education Trends:_

> Why do teens and college students feel entitled to hold an opinion on everything, indict their parents, sit in judgment over authorities?
>
> Television viewing may be a significant part of the answer. This present generation of college students is the first with life-long TV exposure.
>
> Speaking in Toronto on "Children and Television," one authority likened the current situation to that of children in a primitive tribe on a Pacific Island. For children there experience everything that the tribe is doing. Nothing is "classified information." They see everything that everyone is doing in the tribe. The children are everywhere. There are no secrets. There is no privacy.[2]

Think about it: through the TV screen they have been exposed to everything in life—all the marriage problems, all kinds of violence—from intimate bedroom scenes to the whole world situation. They know a great deal, intellectually—but emotionally, it's very difficult for them. I think they need compassion more than any other generation of young people.

I'd like to say this to young people: Remember that you may have information, but this does not necessarily mean you have wisdom. There is something of wisdom that only years can give. Learn to sit down and look into the eyes of gray-haired people, and find out what life is all about!

There are both problems and opportunities in the home today. How are you going to make all this work out? There is only one way. Ephesians 5:21 gives the answer to husbands, wives, children, to everyone: "Submitting to one another in the fear of Christ." We have to adjust ourselves in the home to our proper role, our proper place of responsibility.

Remember, Jesus said we are not to be judging others. "Do not judge" (Matt. 7:1). He says that a judgmental attitude is like a person having a big plank of wood in his eye, saying to somebody, "Let me help you take that speck out of your eye." You know what the person with the speck is going to say? "No, thanks."

Jesus tells you to come to your family relationships with deep humility. In Galatians 5:13–16, we have a good word on this thought: "For you are called to freedom, brothers; only don't use this freedom as an opportunity for the flesh, but serve one another through love. For the entire law is fulfilled in one statement: 'you shall love your neighbor as yourself.' But if you bite and devour one another, watch out, or you will be consumed by one another. I say then, walk by the Spirit and you will not carry out the desire of the flesh."

Call a moratorium on this biting and devouring in the home! Say, "No more! In our home we're going to respect and love each other. We are not going to be critical." And then go to God with your own sins. "If we confess our sins, He is faithful and righteous to forgive us our sins and to cleanse us from all unrighteousness" (1 John 1:9).

My friend, bend low, and go to the cross. Confession is not only vertical toward God, but it's horizontal toward those whom you offend. If you've been like a porcupine to your children, then go to them and tell them that. God will build unity in your home.

My friend, go to work on yourself, by the Spirit of God. Let Him make you into that gentle and loving wife; into that forthright and strong man; into the obedient, kindly young person you want to be. How do you do it? By coming to the cross and admitting that in yourself you can't! And then by drawing your strength from Christ.

We all feel uncertain in our homes. We've seen too many supposedly happy and wonderful homes shaken right to the foundations. Indeed, sometimes our own homes have been shaken. We know that it takes the grace of God to have a happy home.

Come together to the cross. There let Christ work unity into your family. This will give you a taste of heaven on earth!

COMMITMENT THREE:

Commit Yourself to This Needy World

If you could shrink the whole world of people down to just 100 in number, out of the 100 there would be:

57 Asians,

21 Europeans,

14 from the Western Hemisphere, both North and
    South America, and

8 Africans.

52 would be female; 48 would be male.

70 would be non-white; 30 would be white.

70 would be non-Christians; 30 would be Christians.

6 of them would own 59 percent of the world's
    wealth, and all 6 would be from the United
    States.

80 would live in substandard housing.

70 would be unable to read.

50 would suffer from malnutrition.

1 would be near death; 1 would be near birth.

Only 1 would have a college education.

Only 1 would own a computer.

If you woke up this morning more well than sick, you're more blessed than the million people right now in the world who won't survive this week.

If you've never been in battle, in prison, tortured, or starving, you're ahead of 500 million people living right now in the world.

If you can attend church without fear of harassment, arrest, torture, or death, you're more blessed than three billion people in this world.

If you have food in the refrigerator, clothes on your back, a roof overhead and a place to sleep, you are richer than 75 percent of the world.

If you have money in the bank, money in your wallet, and spare change in a dish someplace, you're among the top 8 percent of the world's wealthy.[1]

Listen to God's mourning in His little Book of Lamentations:

Even jackals offer their breasts
to nurse their young,
but my people have become heartless
like ostriches in the desert.
Because of thirst the infant's tongue
sticks to the roof of its mouth;
The children beg for bread,
but no one gives it to them. (4:3–4)

People groan
as they search for bread;
they barter their treasures for food
to keep themselves alive. (1:11)

Young and old lie together
   in the dust of the streets. (2:21)

"Is it nothing to you, all you who pass by?" (1:12)

Your answer may be, "Yes! Yes! I care! I care!"

I just received an e-mail from a couple of friends who are
missionaries in South Africa. They write that "the law and order
situation in our area is not so different from that of the 'Old Wild
West.'"

But they say that believers in the church where they minister
are making a difference. Here's more of their e-mail: "A couple
without kids go to an HIV/AIDS home for the homeless near us
and collect eight or so HIV-positive kids and bring them to
church and Sunday school, then home for play and pizza. One
four-year-old had her birthday the Sunday of her visit. She'd
been found a week earlier in a hut clinging to her mother who
had been dead for three days. There is trauma here, but there is
the presence of Jesus."

Psalm 96 cries,

Declare [God's] glory among the nations,
   his marvelous deeds among all peoples. . . .
Say among the nations, "The LORD reigns." (vv. 3, 10)

We must—we've just got to! We don't dare get into the
mind-set of God-bless-us-four-and-no-more exclusivism! Or, as
somebody with tongue-in-cheek said it,

We are God's chosen few;
   All the rest are damned.
There's no room in heaven for you;
   We don't want heaven crammed.

I understand it to be true that when that great ocean vessel *Titanic* sank, some of the people in lifeboats actually used their paddles to beat off other people in the water trying to climb in!

You don't want to be like that—but where do you start? How can you make a difference in this desperate world?

Let me suggest three areas of concern:

- the world immediately around you that you connect with personally every day—maybe including your own family;
- the world of your neighborhood, waiting to be affected for Christ by your thoughtful words, gifts, and deeds; your small group; your church;
- the "*world*" world, reachable through your specific prayers and letters to missionaries; through your own participation in your church's outreach, in global mission groups, and in relief organizations; and—most thrilling of all—maybe through your going in person yourself.

chapter eleven
THE WORLD IMMEDIATELY AROUND YOU

Your biggest need so that God can use you to win others to Christ is prayer. Pray specifically yourself, and get others to pray for you.

Awhile back, Anne was discouraged: she hadn't led anyone to know the Lord in a long time. When January came, she said to her small group, "Please pray for my New Year's resolution. I've asked the Lord to help me lead six people to Christ this year." (One every other month—that seemed reasonable.)

Well, January passed, and February, and March, April, and May. By June she was frantic: now it would have to be somebody new every month!

She said to her group, "Have you gals been praying for me or not?" And they confessed they pretty much hadn't, and they promised to get down to business and pray for her about it.

A few days later Anne was on her way to teach her usual weekly women's Bible class. She was short on time and hadn't had lunch, so she ducked into a coffee shop and sat down at the counter for a bowl of soup.

A woman on the stool next to her said, "I'm new in town so I have to ask a lot of questions. Do you happen to know if there are any women's Bible classes in this area?"

Anne told her she was just on her way to teach one! The woman followed her in her car, sat through the class, came another time or two, and then was gloriously converted!

This was Jeanne Tkach, who immediately had the gift of evangelism that Anne didn't have. Jeanne led several of her friends to Christ, her dry cleaning man, and her own husband, George, who became the only man in the weekly Bible class!

Anne's small group was thrilled over God's speedy answer to their prayers. They kept on praying, and by year's end God had used Anne to bring six new believers into His family.

Prayer is key—your own and others'. Get serious about this! Before you can connect with the world, you must connect with God.

John 21:3 gives us an insight, here: "'I'm going fishing,' Simon Peter said to [the other disciples]. 'We're coming with you,' they told him. They went out and got into the boat, but that night they caught nothing."

Says A. Van Ryn:

They were unsuccessful. What was the matter?

Did they lack ability? No, they knew their job.

Did they lack experience? No.

Leadership? No, Peter had that quality.

Did they lack unity? Oh, no!

Effort? No, they toiled all night long.

They lacked *Him*. "Apart from me you can do nothing" [John 15:5] is the lesson we may well learn from this incident.[1]

This isn't human work, it's God's.

Don't start first with mere techniques for winning your family members, your familiar inner circle of friends, and your acquaintances. You know well enough that you must love them and give them time and care. The Spirit Who is the Creator will pop creative ways into your mind to do that.

Just *remember where they're headed* without Christ. They look great; they're well dressed; they're accepted by this world: *Remember where they're headed.* They're as lost, as hopeless, as a poor Muslim living somewhere in a vermin-infested shack or a pagan animist picking through garbage dumps for something to eat.

Remember where they're headed.

Second Thessalonians 1:7–8 says that God will soon punish with blazing fire "those who don't know God and . . . those who don't obey the gospel of our Lord Jesus."

Rescue the perishing; care for the dying;
Snatch them in pity from sin and the grave![2]

Because of your awareness of the coming fire of judgment, keep the fire of evangelism burning in your heart.

chapter twelve

THE WORLD
OF YOUR
NEIGHBORHOOD

*H*ere's a motto for you: "Today the neighborhood, tomorrow the world!"

You start with the place where you are, where you already have a footing, where you're plugged into the culture. Learn to weep with those who weep and to laugh with those who laugh, to offer a helping hand when they lack or they hurt, becoming all things to all people to win some.

Remember, the gospel of Christ is relevant! Sometimes we Christians are not relevant. We're "out of it"; we become kind of oddballs in society. We begin to talk a different way; we have a kind of angelic language that makes people wonder what kind of freaks we are! We need to talk like ordinary people, share the gospel like ordinary people, and be ordinary people among them—with the power of God's Spirit working through us.

We must love our neighbors, but not their sin. We must love the world, without becoming worldly.

114

Oh, our attitudes! Everything starts with the First Commitment, my friend, Priority One. When you know how safe you are "in Christ," that He's your fortress, your stronghold, your "high tower," your refuge, and that you're completely safe in Him, that nothing happens to you that He doesn't permit for your highest good and His ultimate glory—when you really know that, you can be *in* your neighborhood but not *of* it. You can really reach to love your neighbors without becoming worldly.

Then when little Frankie down the street says bad words, you don't say your kids can't play with Frankie anymore or they might get contaminated. You say, "Children, Frankie needs Jesus. Let's have him for supper sometimes. Let's show him our love. Maybe he could come to Sunday school with you. Be careful to live right and talk right around Frankie, and we'll pray he'll come to know Jesus."

Your neighborhood is your mission field!

And the neighborhood of adults as well.

Now, suppose God the Spirit prospers your witness and some say yes to receive Christ. Then your work has really begun—your happy, wonderful work!

I heard somebody remark recently that having a baby these days costs at least three thousand dollars. Don't kid yourself! It costs at least a hundred thousand to have a baby—maybe far more. Once that baby is born, you're just beginning.

And that's true of bringing new baby Christians into the world. You feed them spiritually, you care for them, you help them grow. It's costly, but it's worth it. And Jesus says that's what we're to do.

Some of His last words on earth were His marching orders, found in Matthew 28:18–20. After proclaiming that He has all authority He said, "Go . . . and make disciples." Not get decisions and then walk away, but make disciples.

In the city of London, two people died about the same time. One was one of Europe's best-dressed women, and she left a wardrobe of a thousand dresses. The other was a man who left one blue suit, with red on the collar. But he left literally thousands of disciples, who, like him, gave themselves to the poor and friendless of this world. He was William Booth, founder of the Salvation Army.

Lorne Sanny tells about praying over a hostile letter he'd received from a neighbor. The idea came to him that he should invite the neighbor to lunch. Lorne says, "I'm not naturally drawn to having lunch with somebody who's mad at me—but I invited him and he accepted—that day!"

Here's Lorne's story:

> We gave our orders to the waitress, she left, and he turned to me, his lip quivering. "I'm sorry I wrote you that letter, Lorne. I seem to be filled with hostility. My wife and I don't talk. My grown children don't come to visit. Everywhere I go I seem to have a little war on. I need help."
>
> I started meeting with him weekly, helped him establish a quiet time, started him in Scripture memory, beginning with Ephesians 4:30–32. Soon he began to make things right. His blood pressure came down. His wife began communicating. His kids began coming home. And the wars died down.[1]

If I ask you, "Do you really believe in Jesus?" probably you'd say, "Oh, yes, with all my heart." Then I'd ask, "Are you discipling anyone?" And you might say, "Oh, I don't know how to do that." My wife, Anne, has a book, *Love Me with Stubborn Love,*[2] that provides you with plenty of how-to's. Get serious and get a copy from us! Our Web site and address are at the end of this book—and, dear Lord, may that not sound too commercial!

Friend, however inept you may feel, however weak you may feel, just begin by saying, "I start where I am, full of weaknesses and full of troubles in my own life, but nevertheless I have faith that God can possibly, just possibly, use me."

Yes, He can—and He will!

Commit yourself to your neighborhood.

At the end of your life, don't leave behind dresses—leave disciples!

chapter thirteen
THE "WORLD" WORLD

❖ ❖

*N*ow we come to all those people out there—those people who talk funny languages and maybe wear funny hats—whom you never ever expect to meet in person. You'll see a very few of them on television, and since September 11, 2001, they may look dangerous to you, or at least dirty or frightened, seeming to stare as if they've never seen a camera before.

Well, they're so far *away;* shall we just keep them there and not think about them? Jesus' disciples would have agreed. They said in Luke 9:12: "Send the crowd *away.*"

But Jesus Himself, "When He saw the crowds, . . . felt compassion for them, because they were weary and worn out, like sheep without a shepherd" (Matt. 9:36).

God so loves the world—the world of *people.* The Book of Acts is passionately evangelistic! Have you ever noticed how it's peppered with the words *the people?* God has such a concerned heart for "the people"!

3:9: "All the people saw him walking and praising God."

3:11: "All the people [were] greatly amazed."

4:1: "Now as [Peter and John] were speaking to the people, . . ."
4:2: "They were teaching the people. . . ."
4:21: "The people were all giving glory to God. . . ."
5:12: "Signs and wonders were being done among the
    people. . . ."
5:13: "The people praised them highly."

See how Wisdom cries out to *the people* in the Book of
Proverbs:
 [She] calls aloud in the street,
    she raises her voice in the public squares;
 at the head of the noisy streets she cries out,
    in the gateways of the city she makes her
    speech. (1:20–21)

And the Lord Jesus groaned over *people:* "O Jerusalem!
Jerusalem that kills the prophets and stones those who are sent to
her [just as many countries today treat those who bring them the
gospel]! How often I wanted to gather your children together, as a
hen gathers her chicks under her wings, yet you were not willing"
(Matt. 23:37).

And how aggressively the apostle Paul went after the souls of
people: "While Paul was . . . in Athens, his spirit was troubled within
him when he saw that the city was full of idols. So he reasoned . . .
in the marketplace every day with those who happened to be
there" (Acts 17:16–17).

A. B. Simpson, founder of the Christian and Missionary
Alliance, once was entertaining as a houseguest F. B. Meyer, another
"great" of that same generation. Meyer got up early in the morning and tiptoed downstairs to have his quiet time. The study door
was ajar, and there at his desk sat Mr. Simpson, unaware that his
guest was watching him.

Simpson was sitting before a large globe of the world, and he
had his finger on a certain spot, and he was praying. Then he

turned the globe a little, put his finger on another spot, and prayed. He fingered another spot, and prayed. . . .

And then as Meyer watched unnoticed, Simpson leaned forward, took the whole globe in his arms, and hugged it—and *wept*.

Soon the people in this needy world around us will all be gone. And so will you. *Only we people living today can reach these people living today!*

•   Lake Avenue Church in Pasadena, which I pastored for twenty years, has a five-year plan in place. Under their present senior pastor, Gordon Kirk, and their missions pastor, Roger Bosch, each of the five thousand members is hopefully participating in some kind of cross-cultural outreach—from ministry to new California immigrants to covering the globe. This past summer season, for instance, four hundred members fanned out with the precious gospel to seventeen different countries.

Regardless of size, could your church do that?

•   Two months ago, as a member of the board of directors of LIFE Ministries in Japan, I traveled with others to Mongolia (and another country I can't identify) to survey new areas where, under the new name of Asian Access, we're pushing westward. I took along Clint Knox, a young brother out of one of my discipling groups of guys, to expose him to this new thrust for Christ. Sharp Clint and his beautiful Amanda are open to however God wants to use their lives in this world.

Like these two, are you open?

•   Even as I write, our pastor son, Ray Jr., with one of his elders, is in Ethiopia ministering comfort and teaching refugee Sudanese pastors, whom the ruling Muslims of Sudan have driven out (besides actually killing more than two million other non-Muslim Sudanese).

Are you a pastor or teacher who could do that?

• A few years back, Anne and I lived for three months in Kabul, Afghanistan. Then, too, any Afghan who turned from Islam to Christ was tortured and killed—but the outside world was oblivious. War always brings the searchlight of exposure! Worldwide awareness is causing much prayer and Christian strategizing to focus on this area of *the people*—millions of suffering Afghans.

Would you pray? Or join those who strategize?

• Our daughter, Sherry, and her husband, Walt Harrah, have connected with I.S.I. (International Students Incorporated) and "adopted" a foreign couple studying at a university nearby. This young husband and wife from China joined our family recently for Thanksgiving dinner. Walt gave them a Chinese Bible—they'd never seen one before—and the fellow said, "One of the things we want to do in America is study more about Christ." The way he pronounced it, it rhymed with "kissed."

Is there a college near you? You could probably do the same.

• Our Armenian-American friend Steve Lazarian, a very successful businessman, takes other Armenian-Americans in teams with him to minister in Armenia where they found orphanages for homeless children, initiate radio and TV stations to broadcast the gospel, etc. (Years ago we had taken him and his wife, Iris, to be our ministry team in Taiwan.)

Could you help out your former homeland?

• Do you have lots of money? Friends of ours, Peter and Gail Ochs, have several foundations and a staff to roam the world to seek out needs they can finance.

Are you looking for ways to share your wealth?

• Are you a middle-incomer? Our tax man, John Perry, says there are Christian foundations where you can set up a personal account and give from it as you're able.
Are you doing what you can with what you have?

• Do you not have much money? Another dear friend, Fred Dixon, in his eighties, who lives near us in Los Angeles, regularly joins several others in filling a big truck with produce left over from food markets and then making trips to Mexico to give it out in Jesus' name.
You probably live near a poor area. Could you do that?

• For years Anne's mother taught a Bible class and got the attendees not only to learn the Bible but to make World Vision kits and sponsor orphans.
Should you check out World Vision or something like it?

• The Evangelical Free Church of Tempe, Arizona, pours all its money, prayers, and manpower into one Muslim country (which we can't name). Now, there's focused power!
Can you get your church to adopt a country?

• Some of our other friends—doctors, dentists, and lawyers—sometimes take off several months at a time and pay their own way to offer their services free to the poor abroad.
Are you a professional who could do the same?

• There are local outlets that take donated clothes and send them to the poor or to a mission group that sends them overseas.
Do you have extra clothes that you can send?

• For many years before he died, our friend Al Dickson witnessed and counseled several times a week at a local jail.
Should you do that?

• Many people are needed, short term, to go overseas and dig wells or teach English or build buildings.

Or do you have a desk job and gifts that could be used overseas, to release missionaries to do their unique work?

• Mission organizations need prayer and support.

Are you supporting missionaries? Ask for their newsletters so you can stay current on what's happening and how to pray.

• Everywhere we go to mission fields, we see career missionaries who are there for life, middle-agers who've recently gotten on board, or seniors who've arrived for their retirement years and are greatly loved and appreciated.

Is the Holy Spirit tugging at you? Should you go and give your life? Is He also tugging at your spouse, or whoever else would be involved?

Here's one of the great hymns of Christianity's history:
Ye Christian heralds, go proclaim
  Salvation through Immanuel's Name;
In distant climes the tiding bear,
  And plant the Rose of Sharon there.
God shield you with a wall of fire,
  With flaming zeal your hearts inspire;
Bid raging winds their fury ease,
  And hush the tempests into peace.
And when our labors all are o'er
  Then we shall meet to part no more—
Meet with the blood-bought throng to fall
  And crown our Jesus Lord of all![1]

chapter fourteen
LIVE BY PRIORITIES

*S*o I've talked to you about three commitments, three priorities.

They're not priorities made up by Anne and me; they're not an "Ortlund thing."

This is the heart of God! Look at Jesus' prayer in John 17. That chapter is the awesome recording of a lengthy discussion when God the Son talked to God the Father—and He let us humans in on it! This exposure is like nothing anywhere else in all the writings of the world.

So when God talks to God, what does He let us in on that He talks about? His heart is filled with three areas of concern:

- Verses 1–5: The glory of the Father and the glory of the Son.
- Verses 6–19: The well-being of believers.
- Verses 20–26: The conversions of unbelievers.

And, my friend, if your heart is to be in sync with God's heart—if you want your life to have eternal value—these must be your three areas of concern too:

- Love the Triune God and His glory!
- Love, look after, and build up your fellow believers!
- Love and seek the lost, by every means possible!

Some of Jesus' parting words to His disciples just before His crucifixion were these three commands, given in John 15:
- Verses 1–11: "Abide in Me."
- Verses 12–17: "Love one another."
- Verses 18–27: "Testify to the world."

These three priorities are for every Christian, young and old; for every small group; for every church; for every missions organization. Whoever you are, concentrate on putting God first, loving each other, and reaching for this needy world!

These priorities aren't American; they're transcultural.

They're not twenty-first century; they're timeless.

They certainly don't encompass every facet of Christian truth, but they are basic, bottom-line Christianity. They can focus and direct every Christian, anywhere, at anytime.

And they can keep any believer or any church or mission from getting distracted and weakened by too much stuff that's secondary—often even faddish.

I have in front of me notes from my preaching in Pfedelbach, Germany, in 1981:

> This is a truth you keep growing into; you never get to the place where you know all about it. [Oh, my, I think how my life has been refocused and reshaped by these three priorities since 1981!]

> What I know about living with the Body of Christ now is not all that I will know five years from now [or twenty years, Ray Ortlund!].

Maybe your heart has leapt up here and there as you read these words, and you've thought, *I ought to shape up. I ought to take a new look at where I'm going, how my life is turning out. I'm beginning to believe I could be far more than I dreamed.*

My friend, don't put this book down until you've done just that. Have some new thoughts about your life.

You *can* be far more than you dreamed.

You *can* stand before God (listen, that moment isn't far off!) and joyfully receive His rewards for a life well lived. "For we must all appear before the judgment seat of Christ, so that each may be repaid for what he has done in the body, whether good or bad" (2 Cor. 5:10).

You get just one whack at life. There are no reruns. You get just one pass through. You can't ever turn back the clock; all you have left is from here on.

Believe—really believe—that God has answers for you that maybe you didn't even see until now. He promises in Isaiah 42:16:

I will lead the blind by ways they have not known,
        along unfamiliar paths I will guide them;
I will turn the darkness into light before them
        and make the rough places smooth.
These are the things I will do;
        I will not forsake them.

God helps producers for Him to get their lives sorted out. They eliminate in order to concentrate. They set up priorities and put on blinders.

Said former Chrysler head Lee Iacocca: "The main thing is to keep the main thing the main thing."

Are you a little queasy? Do you wonder if you'd become a religious fanatic? George Santayana wrote, "Fanaticism consists of redoubling your efforts when you've forgotten your aim."

Look, you're to aim at God in Christ! You're to keep your eyes on Him and His plan for your individual life. That's not fanaticism;

that's just living "on target." That's cutting out the clutter. That's "in everything" letting Christ "have first place" (see Col. 1:18).

Right now, prayerfully make some plans—just between you and God—deciding two things:

- First, decide what you're going to do.
- Second, decide what you're not going to do.

Doesn't that sound simple?

First, decide what you really want most to do—your top priorities in three areas: toward Christ, toward His Body, and toward the world Christ died to save.

Let's be completely practical. If you're going to think through your life goals, next week is a definable chunk of your life. You could do things next week that would move you on your way to accomplishing all those life dreams.

> It's hard
> By the yard,
> But a cinch
> By the inch.

Take a piece of paper and mark it off like this: under a left-hand column of priorities, write down your own personal "God goals"—maybe several—then your "fellow-believer" goals, then your "world" goals—your work in this world, your witness to it. I can't tell you what these should be, but you and the Lord can work them out. They'd certainly include worship at church and daily Bible study and prayer. They would include fellowship with and ways to encourage the Body, as well as goals of evangelism, giving, and excellence in work and living before unbelievers.

Be specific. You may put down,

I want a daily quiet time.

I want to tithe (that is, give the Lord 10 percent of your income).

I want to learn the art of genuine worship in church—maybe through reading *Up with Worship?*[1]

I want to ask three certain people if they'd like to meet with me weekly for Bible study, prayer, and accountability.

I want to pray with my spouse at least five times a week.

I want to lead my kids in regular prayer and Bible study.

I want to see the Kline family next door won to Christ (by year's end?).

I want to explore one of the missions possibilities in this book that grabbed my heart.

Then on the rest of the sheet, make columns for each weekday and block in the time or times when you're going to help these goals happen.

Next week make another schedule.

Anne and I were helped in all this one time when we read *Up the Organization,* that great little book written by the president of Avis Rent-a-Car. ("We're number two; we try harder.") When he first took over as president, he said, "We're going to define our objective." (I have a strong hunch that very few Christians have ever sat down with pencil and paper and said, "I'm going to define my life's objective"!)

It took six months for Avis, and when the dust settled they had come up with twenty-three words: "We want to become the fastest growing company with the highest profit margin in the business of renting and leasing vehicles without drivers."

They put this statement up everywhere—in all the offices, on all the desks. Immediately it became obvious that they'd have to get rid of some branches of the company that didn't fit: "We're going to get rid of everything that doesn't fulfill this. We're going to put blinders on our eyes to everything else."

You know the success story that resulted.

Anne and I have made a life-purpose statement as a couple:
Our desire is to magnify the Lord and exalt His
name together. [Paraphrased from Ps. 34:3. I proposed
to Anne with this verse, and it's been our basic
together-goal all our married life.] He has burdened
the two of us with the need for renewal, and we purpose to magnify and exalt Him specifically by being
agents of revival among younger Christian leaders and
bodies of believers both at home and abroad. We want
to "serve God's purpose in our own generation" [par-
aphrased from Acts 13:36].

When the two of us together disciple small groups of young
couples, we have them each forge their own purpose statement and
frame it to be seen in their homes.

Second, decide what you're *not* going to do.
All nature has a sloughing-off process.
And so must you, because your life keeps accumulating! Most
Christians are on the run, living busy-busy, pressured lives. Then an
exciting new project is presented to them: "Will you do so-and-
so?" And they gasp, "Oh, I couldn't! I'm too busy. I'm too tired!"
What they really mean is, "My life is fat and slow and clogged with
too many activities, too much clutter."

What they need is a big back door and a big front door, to
continually get rid of and continually take in. "If anyone is in
Christ," says 2 Corinthians 5:17, "he is a new creation; [now, the
Greek verbs in the rest of this verse actually mean continuous
action] the old has gone, the new has come!"

When fresh, lean Christians are presented with a new opportunity, they react, "Wow! A new adventure with the Lord! What
should go so that I can do it?"

By the sixth chapter of Acts, the church had grown so fast that the leaders had to say, "What must go, that we can do well what's most important?" So they handed off the feeding program to others so that they could give themselves to prayer and the ministry of the Word.

They eliminated this to concentrate on that. They stayed lean! Now think carefully, Christian. What should you eliminate to reach your dreams?

The Living Bible version of 1 Corinthians 9:24–25 says this: "In a race, everyone runs but only one person gets first prize. So run your race to win. To win the contest you must deny yourselves many things that would keep you from doing your best."

Maybe you say, "My job itself is just too demanding. Another ten years and I'll have it made, or I can let up a little, but right now, that's just the way it is."

Friend, if you're too busy for God, you're too busy! If you're too busy to attend to the needs of your wife or husband, you're too busy! If your job keeps you from being a good parent to your kids, quit your job! Find something else.

Work—unless it's full-time ministry—has to be part of Commitment Three! Work is tent-making. It's paying the bills so that you can get on to the real business of God and people.

So you've listed your priorities and goals.

Anybody can make a list. It's like quitting smoking: "It's easy; I've done it a hundred times!"

The point is, *what are you going to quit in life to get these priorities accomplished?*

Your danger and mine is not that we become criminals, but rather, that we become respectable, decent, commonplace, mediocre Christians. No rewards at the end, no glory—"saved; yet it will be like an escape through fire" (1 Cor. 3:15)!

The twenty-first-century temptations that really sap our spiritual power are the television, banana cream pie, the easy chair, and the credit card. Christian, you will win or lose in those seemingly innocent little moments of decision.

Pray this with me: "Lord, make my life a miracle!"

And then let us hear from you!

We're at www.ortlund.org. Or write to:

Ray and Anne Ortlund
Renewal Ministries
4500 Campus Drive, Suite 662
Newport Beach, California 92660

NOTES

Chapter One
1. Thomas Kelly, *A Testament of Devotion* (New York: Harper & Brothers, 1941), 115.
2. Brother Lawrence, *The Practice of the Presence of God* (Westwood, N.J.: Fleming H. Revell Company, 1958).
3. Frank C. Laubach, *Letters by a Modern Mystic* (New York: Frank C. Laubach, 1955).
4. Augustus Hopkins Strong, *Systematic Theology* (Fleming H. Revell Company, 1907), 795.
5. Kelly, *A Testament of Devotion*, 114.
6. Thomas Kelly, *The Eternal Promise* (New York: Harper & Row, 1966).
7. For more on this crucial subject, see Ray and Anne Ortlund, *In His Presence* (San Jose: iUniverse, 2001).

Chapter Two
1. Thomas Kelly, *A Testament of Devotion* (New York: Harper & Brothers, 1941), 35.
2. F. W. M. Myers, *Saint Paul* (London: Simpkin, Marshall, Hamilton, Kent, and Company, Ltd., 1916), 13.
3. Kelly, *A Testament of Devotion*, 117.
4. Thomas Kelly, *The Eternal Promise* (New York: Harper & Row, 1966), 54.
5. Brother Lawrence, *The Practice of the Presence of God* (Westwood, N.J.: Fleming H. Revell Company, 1958).
6. Ibid.
7. Harriet Beecher Stowe, hymn "Still, Still with Thee."

8. Kelly, *The Eternal Promise,* 115.

9. For more about this see Anne Ortlund, *Fix Your Eyes on Jesus* (San Jose: iUniverse, 2001).

Chapter Three

1. V. Raymond Edman, *Devotions Are a Delight* (Oradell, N.J.: American Tract Society).

2. William M. Runyan, hymn "Lord, I Have Shut the Door."

Chapter Four

1. Anne Ortlund, *Up with Worship* (Nashville: Broadman and Holman Publishers, 2001), 33–34.

2. This lovely prayer is not only found in the Episcopal Church's *Book of Common Worship,* but it reaches back to *The Cloud of Unknowing* (author unknown), a fourteenth-century devotional classic (New York: Harper and Brothers, 1948), 11.

3. Ortlund, *Up with Worship,* 33–34.

4. Watchman Nee, *What shall This Man Do?* (Ft. Washington, Pa.: Christian Literature Crusade, 1965), 113.

5. Mary A. Lathbury, hymn "Break Thou the Bread of Life."

Chapter Five

1. Bruce Larson, *Setting Men Free* (Grand Rapids: Zondervan Publishing, 1967), 119.

2. Ibid., 119–20.

Chapter Six

1. Anne and I feel so strongly about all this that we've written a new book on this subject: Ray and Anne Ortlund, *A Fresh Start for Your Friendships* (Ann Arbor, Mich.: Servant Publications, 2001).

Chapter Eight

1. Alvin Toffler, *Future Shock* (New York: Random House, 1970), 211.

2. Marvin R, Vincent, *Word Studies in the New Testament* (New York: Charles Scribner's Sons, 1887, 1915), Volume I, 650.

Chapter Nine

1. J. H. Jowett, *The Epistles of St. Peter* (New York: A.C. Armstrong & Son, 1906), 109.

Chapter Ten

1. W. J. Fields, *Unity in Marriage* (St. Louis: Concordia Publishing House, 1962), 41–42.

2. *Christian Education Trends* (Elgin, Ill.: David C. Cook Publishing), 2 September 1968.

Commitment Three

1. Philip, M. Harter, MD, FACEP, Stanford University, School of Medicine.

Chapter Eleven

1. Keswick calendar, December 2, year unknown.

2. Fanny Crosby, hymn "Rescue the Perishing."

Chapter Twelve

1. "The Equipper," a newsletter put out by Lorne Sanny, chairman of the U.S. board of directors of the Navigators, 19 May 1988.

2. Anne Ortlund, *Love Me with Stubborn Love* (Lincoln: iUniverse, 2000).

Chapter Thirteen

1. Bourne H. Draper, hymn "Ye Christian Heralds," 1803.

Chapter Fourteen

1. Anne Ortlund, *Up with Worship* (Nashville: Broadman and Holman Publishers, 2001).

P.S. In your thinking, please omit the paragraph at the bottom of page 131: Life has changed!

How about committing yourself with a response – sort of joining an on-going "Company of the Committed"?

Dr. Ray Ortlund, Sr., is now in heaven, but Dr. Ray Ortlund, Jr., has taken up his dad's legacy, in loving, seamless transition. You can reach him at www.ortlund.org, Renewal Ministries' continuing website.

Or you can write me at
Mrs. Anne Ortlund
601 Lido Park Drive, 6E
Newport Beach, California 92663

Made in the USA
Coppell, TX
21 October 2021